VICTORY:
DESTROY WITCHES AND WITCHCRAFT

ANOINTED PRAYERS THAT BREAK EVERY YOKE

Rev. Tony Ekperechi

This edition first published in paperback by
Michael Terence Publishing in 2024
www.mtp.agency

Copyright © 2023, 2024 Rev. Tony Ekperechi

Rev. Tony Ekperechi has asserted the right to be identified as
the author of this work in accordance with the
Copyright, Designs and Patents Act 1988

ISBN 9781800949225

No part of this publication may be reproduced, stored
in a retrieval system, or transmitted, in any form or
by any means, electronic, mechanical, photocopying,
recording or otherwise, without the prior
permission of the publisher

The Bible texts used in this publication are from the
Kings James Version and the Amplified Version,
otherwise stated

Cover image (AI)
by Michael terence Publishing

Cover design
Michael Terence Publishing
www.mtp.agency

Michael Terence
Publishing

The Ministry

We are here to encourage you and, for you to understand that with God all things are possible. There is no doubt that witches and witchcraft exist, even the Bible acknowledges that and decreed that we should not allow them to live. Whatever you reject on earth is rejected in heaven. Your word is the word of God provided you are on the right cause.

Exodus 22:18 says, "Thou shalt not suffer a witch to live." In other words, whatever is bound on earth shall be in heaven. Meaning that the moment you bind them here, your prayer is assured in heaven. On the other hand, if you allow them to cage you with fear and doubts as to their powers and what they can do, then there you are.

We are here to teach you so that you do not fear them; and or believe in their powers. The Christ in you is greater than them and their evil works. You have overcome them with the blood of the lamb, and the words of your testimonies. As you navigate through this book, it will build your faith and create in you a new spirit that overcomes all the powers of the enemies and the evil ones.

Guideline

"Now unto him, that can do exceedingly abundantly above all that we ask or think, according to the power that worketh in us." Ephesians 3:20 (KJV).

It is easier to receive when you believe God can do it for you and not just with your strength. You stand to waste time if you doubt. The Hebrews spent forty years in the wilderness because they refused to believe God or the promises concerning them.

If you believe that He can do it for you then your faith has taken you through. The power that works in you is the amount of faith you have and the ability to increase your faith with prayer and positive thinking, meditations, visualisations, and confessions.

Believe Him and see His glory in your life, even beyond and above your imagination and expectations. Praise God!!

Dedication

This book is dedicated to Jesus and the Kingdom Temple. It is He and the Kingdom Temple Pentecostal Ministry team that, encouraged me to publish it. Without Jesus and the Ministry, it would not have been possible to publish it.

Printed and Published by Kingdom Temple Pentecostal Ministries 2024, for the Conquerors.

www.dficc.co.uk

The Bible texts used in this publication are from the Kings James and Amplified versions, otherwise stated.

All rights reserved. No part of this book shall be reproduced or transmitted in any form or by any means, electronic or mechanical, including photocopying, recording, or by any information media without the written permission of the publishers.

Useful Quotations

"For if the trumpet gives an uncertain sound, who shall prepare himself for battle?" I Corinthians 14:8 (KJV).

"A man's mind plans his way: but the Lord directs his steps and makes them sure." Proverbs 16:9 (AMP).

"Be careful of nothing, but in everything by prayer and supplication with thanksgiving let your request be made known unto God." Philippians 4:6 (KJV).

"The earth is the Lord's, and the fullness thereof; the world, and they that dwell therein." Psalms 24:1 (KJV).

"A reproof enters deeper into a man of understanding than a hundred lashes into a [self-confident] fool." Proverbs 16:10 (AMP).

"For who hath known the mind of the Lord that he may instruct him? But we have the mind of Christ." I Corinthians 2:16 (KJV).

Acknowledgements

Thank God for my family, Pastor Ama Alaike, for their kind support throughout the writing of this book.

May God bless them abundantly for their efforts. Amen.

We pray for our Editor, Miss Favour Nkemjika Ekperechi for her unflinching support and dedication to the Ministry for greater grace, wisdom, knowledge and understanding to continue in the right part of the Lord to achieve greater success in the mighty name of Jesus, amen.

Rev. Tony Ekperechi.

Contents

Introduction 1
1: Symptoms of Witchcraft and What to Do 7
2: Imaginations...28
3: Casting Down Imaginations 49
4: A Man Reaps What He Sows 75
5: Victory 80
6: The Heart of Man 105
7: The Power in the Blood of Jesus............................120
8: Destroying the Power of the Witches 131
9: Evil Plans Cannot Stand...139
10: Targeted Prayers...141
    They Shall Come to Nought 141
    Prayer Against Evil Devices 142
    Prayer Against Fastened Nails 143
    Trample on Snakes and Scorpions 145
    A New Person...147
    Prayer Against the Witches.................................151

Introduction

This book will help you to understand the meaning of victory, how to get the victory; and maintain it without losing it. As a victor, you learn how to use your imagination, your mind's eyes, and your spiritual eyes to see what others cannot see. Understand when you are held up by evil spirits or evil people or held up by yourself due to the way you think or the choices you make.

You are created in victory, born in victory and the victory of God is in you. Your mindset, belief system, and attitude will determine your focus and how you see and handle matters. It will also determine how quickly you can achieve your victory, and how far and well you can go.

It will also teach you to know when the battle is inside you and whether you are imagining those things in your mind. That's because Satan can put fear in your mind and you begin to see fear and think that it is real when in fact it's false, denigration and lies. Apart from imagination, a positive thinker is a philosopher who sees no limits in his mind, an achiever who believes that all things are possible, and where others fail, he will succeed, while a negative thinker is the reverse.

As a man thinketh in his heart, so is he. This book will encourage you to adopt the right mental attitude to life to achieve, using the appropriate words where necessary while making your confessions and affirmations. Your life is centred on your thoughts, imagination, attention, focus, meditations, and affirmations. We will teach you how to guide your mind to think in the right ways and manner.

It will encourage you to take the necessary authority from the Word of God to trample on the works and powers of the witches and other enemies who may want to attack or disrupt your plans in life. The enemies are wise, but the wisdom from God is greater than theirs. As a result, you will be spiritually discerned to understand the plans or devices of your enemies and how to stop them. To be forewarned is to be forearmed.

If you know ahead of them, what they are planning, you will ensure they will only try and fail. It also deals with how the blood of the Lamb can protect you and your family from evil attacks. The blood of the Lamb will protect you from harm. When the enemies see the blood, they shall Passover.

When and how you can cover your family and properties with the blood, and when the evil spirits see the blood, they will Passover. This book will teach you how the name of Jesus can be used so that all other spirits will bow. Because He is a strong Tower and the Lord of lords and at the mention of this name every knee must bow, and every tongue confesses that He is Lord! (Philippians 2:10-11). The name of the Lord is also a strong tower, the righteous run into it and are saved (Proverbs 18:10).

Some people cannot move forward in life instead they move backwards, and any young person will overtake them. Others move slowly, others go around in the circle, and some standstill. This book will teach you to understand if it is the work of the enemies and who may be responsible for your plight. Some people can do evil to others, but the Lord has anointed us to come to your aid or assistance.

Even your unfriendly friends and brothers will confess to you knowingly and unknowingly what they have been doing to you. You will also learn how to use your dreams to solve problems. If you live, move, and have your being in the Word of God which is in Christ, then you will live a more peaceful and fruitful life, even beyond what you can imagine or think of.

Witchcraft is an evil mind and evil imagination. It is the attraction of negative energy or spirit. It is casting a spell on someone or causing him not to excel or prosper and sometimes, kill him. It is causing someone to continue to rotate in circles or fall backwards. It is causing a son of light to walk and dwell in darkness, destiny, or life stolen.

As a result of his evil mind, you become filled with, negative energies and a lack of clarity and focus. They do not know what to do next, where they are heading and how to get help. Of course, they knew that if you get help, you shall be free from them and their afflictions.

The main issue is that the victim may not be able to think for himself except when some relatives are willing to help him. Even those who could help may not want to interfere with others' issues and the afflicted may not care about getting help because they are confused.

This book will help you to connect to your inner self which is the Spirit of God in you and flush out all negative energies or spirits in you and you become that original one whom the Lord has blessed and commands to have dominion and reign all over the earth. You are born of God and not of the flesh to reign on Earth because all things are yours.

The Word will direct your affairs and you will not have any problems beyond what you can reasonably handle because the Lord and His heavenly hosts are always on your side and not just on your side but are there with you. Many people are practicing witchcraft without knowing it. He or she does not have to practice or go to evil diviners, sorcerers, enchanters, magicians, or wizards but, is carrying those evils in his heart or mind. The Bible says, 'as a man thinketh in his heart, that is what he is.'

The witches operate in different ways. They may want to take someone's life straight away or steal his destiny so that he will be moving around the circle without achieving anything in life. Remember that if they kill a person or steal his destiny, all the benefits of that person in life will go or be passed over to them both in the physical and spiritual realms while some do not get any benefit from it.

They will put their victim in a state of confusion so that he will not be able to do anything right and not seek help. The more his pain, the more benefits they enjoy. "And David enquired at the Lord, saying, Shall I pursue after this troop? Shall I overtake them? And he answered him, pursue thou shalt surely overtake them, and without fail recover all." 1 Samuel 30:8 (KJV).

Remember that David could not do it by his power, it was the Lord who fought the battle for him and gave him victory to recover all. That same Lord is still with you. Praise God!

Prayer:

- I decree and declare that I chase, overtake, and recover the time, resources, children, husband, wife, money, properties and all that the enemies have stolen from me over the years a trillion times in the mighty name of Jesus.

- I decree and declare that all the atrocities committed against me, and my family be returned to senders a trillion folds in Jesus' mighty name, I pray.

- As they come like a flood, the Lord shall set a standard against them in the mighty name of Jesus.

- When they come like a flood, let the earth open and swallow them as in the days of Moses.

- Any evil altar they have taken our names to, I bind them, rebook them, uproot them, destroy them, set them on fire, and break loose from all their evil manipulations in the mighty name of Jesus. Thank You, Lord, for setting us free in the mighty name of Jesus, amen.

"Finally, brethren, whatsoever things are true, whatsoever things are honest, whatsoever things are just, whatsoever things are pure, whatsoever things are lovely, whatsoever things are of good report; if there be any virtue, and if there be any praise, think on these things. Those things, which ye have both learned, and received, and heard, and seen in me, do and the God of peace shall be with you." Philippians 4:8-9 (KJV).

In conclusion, anything you say, or do will surely come back to you, and even if they are any praises, they will still come to you. Therefore, whatsoever a man sows he shall reap.

Some of us do not know who we are, or why we are where we are. Imagine you are walking or running on a treadmill for hours and sweating, you will end up exercising your body but going nowhere. Imagine you have a destination and, walking to it and not going anywhere. Then you start to run and cannot go faster than a snail's pace.

As you are not moving or too slow, you decide to go by bicycle and nothing changes. As you are not getting corresponding results for your efforts, you decide to go by car and still get the same results. As the result was not encouraging, you went on a superbike or supercar, still the same result and burning more gas.

Given these challenges, you refused to give up because quitters do not win. You decide to jet off, but your aeroplane managed to take off but was burning gas without flying anywhere. The pilot wondered and returned to the airport. While investigating, you confessed that you have been going through that, and whatever you tried never moved or flourished.

The management left you out and flew other passengers and the journey or flight was smooth. Jona had a similar experience and the solution was found. Therefore, it is set time to favour zion.

Have you tried to find out what is going on in your life and what is responsible? Remember too that some people excel where all others fail.

Those times you spent walking to nowhere, running to nowhere, biking to nowhere, driving to nowhere, or jetting off to nowhere are times lost that cannot be regained. Time is the only resource that cannot be regained because any minute, hour, day, week, month or year lost becomes history and cannot be gained back.

Notice employees are paid by time, the skilled are paid according to their skills plus their hourly input while the contractors charge for materials plus the time input. Therefore, time is hugely the essence or substance of all things.

Understanding your dreams is very important. Things often start going wrong when they see themselves walking in the flood, in the bushes, and sometimes on bush paths. These people often find themselves walking in darkness, doing long walks, without end and missing their way in the dream. Being chased, and fighting even with masquerades, they see or fight with snakes and scorpions, cats, and dogs, lose money, dream deaths, have near-miss accidents, offered poisonous food or drinks. These dreams are often repetitive or recurring. They see and deal with unknown spirits and sometimes with late relatives in their dreams. Whatever they set their hands to do will hardly work out. If you are in this group, please seek help. You cannot do it alone. There are men of God who are anointed to help.

The moment you notice problems or challenges, please seek a solution because this world is not just spiritual but spirit. There is no time in the spirit because everything is now and no tomorrow.

1: Symptoms of Witchcraft and What to Do

The Lord created the earth, made man in His image and likeness, blessed him, and gave man dominion over all He had created. Life is not supposed to be full of challenges and some issues are not supposed to come up. Most of them are manmade out of envy or jealousy. You are not made to suffer so much but at each time of your life, you can face some common issues or processes to prepare you for your next responsibility because life is not stagnant but dynamic.

As is customary or common to man, and at the same time the Lord will make a way out or escape route for you. Everything was prepared for you before your birth. At the same time, it might be necessary to evaluate your life, and those around you, to determine if your life is standing still, moving backwards, or going around the circle or in the spiral.

You must examine your life and know your purpose in life and how to manage them. It is patent to know that your potentiality is infinite without limitation. You can think anything, do anything, and achieve anything in life without limits, that is if you believe.

The most important thing in life is your time. You must; learn to manage it because when it is gone, it is gone for good, and you cannot get it back. Do not allow your enemies to get you to think and act foolishly. In other words, do not allow anybody to detect and control your world or you regret and cry at last.

"And thou mourn at the last, when thy flesh and thy body are consumed, and say, how have I hated instruction, and my heart despised reproof; And have not obeyed the voice of my teachers, nor inclined mine ear to them that instructed me! I was almost in all evil amid the congregation and assembly. Proverbs 5:11-14 (KJV).

Do not allow your precious time to be consumed by your enemies who would keep you busy working without results. Those evil people will also give you names as foolish, failures who cannot achieve anything or coordinate their lives when in fact they are the reason. Do not give them that grace to subdue you. Here are some symptoms of witchcraft:

- A brilliant student cannot pass examinations, whereas the less brilliant ones pass the same exam. This is the work of destiny killers.
- Difficulty getting into higher education or apprenticeship while others with a similar background are getting them. The work of destiny killers.
- Problems getting a job after education or training. The work of destiny killers.
- Having problems in your business or job while others in the same field or occupation are thriving while you are at a standstill. The work of the dream killers.
- When the children are so delinquent; and are not able to do or understand anything. The work of envious relatives.
- Where you have many children in the family; and they cannot get married, particularly the girls. Handwork of the enemies.
- A full-grown man earning income does not want to marry.
- A situation where a person work or does business and is always broke when in fact, he is making money. Devouring spirit, work of the enemies.
- When a person gets sick or unwell when is the time to go to an interview or exams?

- Sudden or untimely death through accidents or some other useless viruses. Work of the enemies.
- Miscarriages and delays in conceptions. Work of the enemies,
- Late marriages particularly among men. Work of the enemies.
- Walking or tracking endlessly in the dreams even in the bush and sometimes you miss your way, typical witchcraft.
- Being unable to coordinate what you are doing or planning is the work of evil people.
- Children dying young. Work of the enemies.
- Confusion, delays and going in circles in life. Work of the enemies.
- No promotion in life even at work. Work of the enemies.
- No favour. Work of the enemies.
- You cannot go to church to seek solutions. Work of the enemies.
- Not having money to seek a solution to your ordeal or tribulation, work of destiny killers.
- Attacks in your dreams.

"According as his divine power hath given unto us all things that pertain unto life and godliness, through the knowledge of him that hath called us to glory and virtue: whereby are given unto us exceeding great and precious promises: that by these ye might be partakers of the divine nature, having escaped the corruption that is in the world through lust." 2 Peter 1:3-4 (KJV).

God is a Spirit, and anything born of God is a spirit. You are born not according to flesh and blood or corruptible, but incorruptible and of the Holy Spirit and power. You have a divine birth and the divine nature of God through the Holy Spirit; and of His Christ the Messiah whom the Lord has sent to reconcile us to Himself.

By giving us the knowledge of Him through whom we are made because many of us do not know who they are because they do not know their Father. How can you know who you are when you do not know your father or who your father is?

You are in the Father and the Father is in you and the gate of hell or witches or evil men cannot prevail. Christ said to Peter, thou art Peter, on this rock, I shall build my church and the gates of hell cannot prevail. Take yourself as Peter or Rock and the gate of hell shall never prevail or overcome you.

Thou art the son of God, the works of the evils cannot prevail or work on you because you are His temple, and His Holy Spirit dwells and rests in you. Your prayers don't seem to have been answered sometimes because those bewitching you are not far from you. You could be living in the same roof with him; therefore, you are monitored spiritually, and physically.

They might be trying to get rid of you, but the Lord is fighting your battle for you and giving you victory without you knowing about it. I pray with you to the Lord to open your eyes to see how you are getting your victories.

A stranger cannot bewitch you except those who are close to you which could be your spouse, relatives, friends, or colleagues; the in-laws and other family friends who are jealous, envious, or threatened by your personality or presence. When you have a manipulator, you are in for a big problem particularly when he feels insecure because as they do it, he will be accusing you of all that he is doing, and you who is the actual victim will be on the defence. The answer is strong faith, fervent prayer and keeping away from such people. "Confess your faults one to another, and pray one for another, that ye may be healed. The effectual fervent prayer of a righteous man availed much." James 5:16 (KJV).

Some people are delivered from serious troubles and illnesses without knowing why and how they are delivered, is because we are praying for them without them knowing about it.

This is not to ask you to go on to attack your friends and relatives, trust the Lord will guide you to avoid such evil people in your life without making mistakes if you pray passionately or ardently and trust in Him. Suppose you read this book and follow the prayers. The Lord will open your eyes to know who you are and who is in your life.

That is why the Lord told the lady at the well, that it is neither on this mountain nor the other, the true worshippers must worship the Father in spirit and truth. Spiritual and truthful worship means understanding who you are and what you are doing and will continue to do. The Lord directs the steps of His chosen.

You are that rock, the stone of ages that cannot deteriorate or die. The resurrecting spirit which brought Christ from death is in you therefore you have overcome with your faith because it is a belief system of a thing. It is your faith, mindset, and belief system that will make you free and Jesus said to her go in peace, your faith has made you whole.

The fact or reality cannot make any person free from a demonic, attack, demonic influence, sickness, or poverty; it is only the truth that is in your visions, aspirations, dreams, imagination, hard work, determination, and focus. The Bible says, 'everything hangs on work.' You work with your faith because it is the Father who gave you the power, knowledge, and energy to create wealth, success, and a good life. "All things are full of labour; man cannot utter it: the eye is not satisfied with seeing, nor the ear filled with hearing. The thing that hath been, it is that which shall be, and that which is done is that which shall be done: and there is no new thing under the sun." Ecclesiastes 1:8-9 (KJV).

You can think and grow rich by performing that reality created through your thought system. They cannot work or manifest without some reasonable level of effort. You conquer evil spirits by tackling and opposing them. The Bible asks you to oppose the devil and he shall flee from you. The devil or witches cannot flee when you stay idle and cry. You must fight back. All things are full of labour or work, and you cannot change it with miracles because miracles are expectations with some level of faith and work.

You are all aware that faith is dead on arrival without work and the Bible cannot lie. Anything which is to be done has been done, those required to be done have been done and those expected to be done have all been done. You cannot change it because all things are done through love. After all, faith works through love and hard work. Your breakthrough is by paying attention through focus and determination to overcome and destroy them. You are of God and in His image and likeness and He has given you the spirit to overcome and even possess the gates of your enemies.

You all have the grace of His glorious knowledge and power to partake in His divine power to make all things possible because with Him nothing is impossible as you are no more of flesh and blood but of a divine nature of God your Father. You have overcome because even if they come as a flood, the Lord shall raise a standard against them in which the Spirit of the Father shall lift you above them. After all, your potentiality is infinity or without measure.

"According to their deeds, accordingly he will repay, fury to his adversaries, recompense to his enemies; to the islands, he will repay recompense. So shall they fear the name of the Lord from the west, and his glory from the rising of the sun. When the enemy shall come in like a flood, the Spirit of the Lord shall lift a standard against him." Isaiah 59:18-19 (KJV).

They cannot work because your faith is that standard that the Lord has set above them. It is a belief system and a mindset. In one of my dreams, there was a flood, and as the water was rising, I was lifted, and this old lady was asking me to come down. I cannot go down because the Lord has raised me with His Spirit and set a standard against them. Therefore, no matter what they do, it shall not work.

We have escaped the corruption of this world through envy, jealousy, fear, and doubts which are the most dangerous ones. Many are destroyed by evil people, because of fears and doubts as to how to engage them or escape from them thus falling into their bondage and enslaving themselves. The wicked can plan and try their evils but they shall not work because only the counsel of the Lord which you have agreed to yourself can work in your life.

Your enemies cannot dictate to you unless you agree with them. The Bible says where two shall agree on anything as touching it shall be done unto them by my Father. In your case, even if there are more than two against you without you agreeing with them it shall not stand because the word of the Master says, 'their gathering will be in vain.' It shall not stand either shall they come to pass, and the fire of the Holy Ghost shall go down and scatter that gathering. Praise God.

Therefore, you are no more an ordinary mortal but immortal, incorruptible, the tent of the Holy Omnipotent God full of grace and truth. When the Lord created the heaven and the earth, He made everything ready before creating the first couple and housed them in a Garden called Eden. In the garden were assorted fruits, animals, rivers, and precious stones such as gold and silver. He then blessed them and asked them to multiply, increase and have dominion over everything that He had created (Genesis 1:26-28).

Let us for example for a man trying to have a family, he will first try to get a job to look after the new family and a home to house them. He should be able to prepare for other eventualities as much as he can like putting away some money for the children's school fees depending on the country and environment.

Life is one that everyone deserves to live a fruitful and fulfilling life, and this book strives to help us achieve that by providing a range of scriptures and prayers that cater to specific individual needs. Our goal is to give you the gospel truth as provided in the scriptures with analysis and reasoned arguments as to why it should or should not be the way it is. There is no failure in life, and no one is created to fail because you are victorious, an overcomer, a conqueror and borne of God.

However, some are more blessed or have greater grace than others but with no intention that someone should fail or suffer in his life. Failure is not an option because it is not from the Lord. His only option is blessing, blessing, blessing, and blessing upon children and children's children. As a result, when things start to go haywire or non-functional, we need to look back and ask why.

Those of us with spiritual eyes can see it immediately even before they begin to come. This world is spiritual, and the Maker of the world is a Spirit and everything that He had created are spirits and are linked to each other including our good selves.

Sometimes, we go through pains and challenges, which are designed to help us to get to the next ladder or dimension. In all cases, there are provisions for removing or handling negative vibes or energies which could distract you. When you find yourself drained, confused, and walking in circles in the wilderness, without hope, and people are calling you names and laughing at you even though they are responsible for your plight. Do not give up, we've been there. It is part of cleansing or purification. You will come out of it triumphantly.

Start that journey of a thousand miles with your first step by looking for help. We are here for you and some other similar organisations and churches. Sometimes, you may not be able to do it alone. The Bible says, 'where two shall agree as touching anything, it shall be done by our heavenly Father.' Praise God!

"Again, I say unto you, that if two of you shall agree on earth as touching anything that they shall ask, it shall be done for them of my Father which is in heaven. For where two or three are gathered in my name, there am I in the midst of them." Matthew 18:19-20 (KJV).

The Lord allows us to go through some of them as part of the process or training so that we can use them to help you so that you can also help others. One good thing about our heavenly Father is that He will not allow any vibes or challenges that we cannot be able to handle to come to us and at the same time, He shall make an escape route for us.

"Therefore, thus saith the Lord, who redeemed Abraham, concerning the house of Jacob, Jacob shall not now be ashamed, neither shall his face now wax pale. But when he sees his children, the work of mine hands, in the midst of him, they shall sanctify my name, and sanctify the Holy One of Jacob, and shall fear the God of Israel." Isaiah 29:23-24 (KJV).

You are sanctified, and there is deliverance and holiness in Israel, the house of Jacob shall possess their possessions. You cannot fail or be shamed; the Lord shall see you through. Therefore, darkness cannot overcome you, the light of God. Just be thoughtful, positive, focused, determined, and attentive which is your meditation that creates your world or reality.

"There hath no temptation taken you, but such as is common to man: but God is faithful, who will not suffer you to be tempted above that ye are able; but will with the temptation also make a way to escape, that ye may be able to bear it." 1 Corinthians 10:13 (KJV). Sometimes you feel trapped, exhausted, and confused with life without knowing what to do or way out. He is faithful in that he will not allow any temptation to overtake you that you cannot cope with and at the same time will make an escape route for you.

The Lord will use us to make that your escape route and we are here to assist you to cope with it successfully and triumphantly and come out of it as He has done for others. They brought a young lady who was going through a mental problem to me. I prayed for her, and she attended our prayer meetings a few times and received prayers.

Along the line, she started knowing where she was and started narrating her stories to me. The most painful thing there was that she was the senior among her siblings, and they respected her not because of her condition.

They bullied, kicked, and slapped her. When evil people try to transmit their evil to get hold of a person, the first place is to take control of the person's subconscious mind, whereby he cannot think, or reason and his brain becomes blurred or distorted. To conclude the long story, the Lord used us to His glory to restore her to the Lord's glory.

The last time I saw her was at the Woolwich market. A pretty girl walked past when I was with the bishop, and he asked if I knew the lady that walked past and I said no. However, I did not look at the person except that I saw a pretty person walk past us and he told me that it was the girl with a mental issue which I prayed for, and the Lord healed her.

I pray that her healing will be complete, and I also pray for you reading this book to receive your healing from whatever challenges you may be facing in Jesus' name, amen. We always and always thank the Lord for His goodness and mercies. Weeping may endure for a night but joy cometh in the morning. The anointing breaks or destroys every yoke. You cannot be defined by misfortune. Praise God!!

If you have the gift of dreams and visions, you will see those responsible for your predicaments saying it in the spirit and repeating the same thing in the physical. The word of God is good for teaching and reproving in righteousness so that a son of God may be competent and complete in every good work.

"All scripture is given by inspiration of God, and is profitable for doctrine, for reproof, for correction, for instruction in righteousness: That the man of God may be perfect, thoroughly furnished unto all good works." 2 Timothy 3:16-17 (KJV).

As Christians, we can deny curses and witchcraft as much as we can, but they are still there. When the Father created the heavens and the earth, the earth was without form and void and filled with water and darkness. In real terms, some people do use mediums to propel themselves in their careers and can also use the same medium to control, monitor and seize a person's destiny.

"And the earth was without form and void, and darkness was upon the face of the deep. And the Spirit of God moved upon the face of the waters." Genesis 1:2 (KJV). Now you can see that darkness was the first thing that appeared when the earth was created. It was not only dark but void meaning emptied and worthless or useless and good for nothing. At the same time, the Lord was there in the dark old sea or waters and His Spirit was moving in the face of the predicament which could be an attack or process.

Know that the Lord is there with you with all His heavenly hosts. Darkness did not depart until the Lord cast it out and later brought it back to become the night, otherwise, it would have been all day without night. You must, therefore, stand up to your enemies, otherwise, they will not depart. "Submit yourselves, therefore, to God. Resist the devil, and he will flee from you." James 4:7 (KJV).

When everything is smooth, you may not bother to remember the Lord who fights your battle and that's why He asks the House of Jacob to remember the Lord when they begin to drink from the wells, they did not dig or live in the houses they did not build (Deuteronomy 6:10-14).

When you are going through a dilemma or thereafter, you should not forget the Lord, your God who gives you victory. "And God said, let there be light: and there was light." Genesis 1:3 (KJV). When He saw the light, He said this is good and He proceeded with His creative activities. He did not end it there, He called darkness back including its vainness and voidness, and called it night and separated it from the light which He calls day.

The night is not meant for creativity and productivity. It is meant for sleeping or idleness, thinking, meditating, reflecting on what is going on in one's life, and time to say no to no and yes to yes. You need light to do something at night, that is why we need electricity and other man-made lights to see or work at night.

The night is voided to carry out any meaningful thing without light hence we use it to sleep and rest and regain lost energy. No one is a failure, but someone very close is responsible for your pain and predicament or plight. With such a predicament, the night becomes the time to cry to the Lord and take authority in heaven and earth and deal with all the works of the enemies and that calls for midnight prayers and stand up to your enemies.

You must recognise that sufferings, failures, and pains are not usually from the Lord, but man's inhuman treatment or affliction to his brothers which could be resisted by knowing the truth which will set you free. The same people will be talking – He cannot do this; he cannot do that. He cannot marry, he cannot pass a common exam, he cannot buy a car, he cannot get a job. He cannot, he cannot, he cannot. Cannot is now his name.

Wherever he goes, they say that is he who cannot. You stand to suffer more if you live with your hater or someone bewitching you under the same roof. Now you must be very careful of who you marry as husband or wife. This is very important because the problem won't end even if you get a divorce particularly when children are involved.

Is that the will of God for you? No! An evil man will afflict evil on you out of envy or for whatever reason or no reason. An evil man does not delight in anything good for anybody even for himself and his family. Some people may mean well for only their family and not others. But where I came from, they think evil and perform evil, and no one moves up. With that, I think seriously about the law of karma, the law of cause and reward or effect, and the law of action and reactions. Whatsoever he sows, that he shall reap.

Witchcraft is an evil mind and evil imagination. It is the attraction of negative energy or spirit. It is casting a spell on someone or causing him not to excel or prosper and sometimes, kill him. It is causing someone to continue to rotate in circles or fall backwards. It is causing a son of light to walk and dwell in darkness, destiny, or life stolen.

As a result of his evil mind, you become filled with, negative energies and a lack of clarity and focus. They do not know what to do, where they are heading and how to get help. Of course, they knew that if you get help, you shall be free from them and their afflictions. The main issue is that the victim may not be able to think for himself except when some relatives are willing to help him. Even those who could help may not want to interfere with others' issues and the afflicted may not care about getting help because they are confused.

This book will help you to connect to your inner self which is the Spirit of God in you and flush out all negative energies or spirits in you and you become that original one whom the Lord has blessed and commands to have dominion and reign all over the earth. You are born of God and not of the flesh to reign in all the earth because all things are yours.

"Therefore, let no man glory in men. For all things are yours; Whether Paul, or Apollos, or Cephas, or the world, or life, or death, or things present, or things to come; all are yours; And ye are Christ's; and Christ is God's." 1 Corinthians 3:21-23 (KJV).

Do not mind whatever they call you. Seek help, you will rise above the storm. They cannot succeed. You have to learn how to break free from them and begin a new life. It is not what they call you that you will be or will become your name. It is what you call you that will make or break you. Your life is in your hands and your heart. It is all about you and your faith and belief system.

Let us look at the story of this man named Legion in the Bible. He was known as Legion because when the Lord asked of his name he answered, 'Legion.' It was not him that answered the Lord; it was the spirits in him. He lost control of his life because those spirits had taken over his mind and he could no longer think, reason or make decisions for himself.

The same thing applies to many people today. "And cried with a loud voice, and said, what have I to do with thee, Jesus, thou Son of the God Most High? I adjure thee by God, that thou torment me not. For he said unto him, Come out of the man, thou unclean spirit. And he asked him, what is thy name? And he answered, saying, my name is Legion: for we are many." Mark 5:7-9 (KJV). See the wicked spirit tormenting a man was begging the Lord not to torment him. That is the wicked world for you. Evil people will not want you to fight back but will quote that Jesus asks you to forgive your enemies while they won't stop.

Now look at this man, how did those demons enter him? Was it because of witchcraft or what? What happened to him and is there anything we can learn from his experience and how the

Lord tackled the demons? I stand to remind you that believers stand in the power and authority to do the same even greater work shall you do. Have you got spiritual eyes?

Do you see with them, if not, can you improve on them and learn how to see with them? Many people are suffering the same thing today. They have many unclean spirits in them, and lost control of the affairs of their lives as a result, and would not seek help, nor do they know how to seek help for themselves.

"Verily, verily, I say unto you, He that believeth on me, the works that I do shall he do also; and greater works than these shall he do; because I go unto my Father. And whatsoever ye shall ask in my name, that will I do, that the Father may be glorified in the Son." John 14:12-13 (KJV).

You can think like Christ and perform those greater miracles because you are gifted and anointed with those great anointing. You are a mighty man of valour which you must learn to know and activate. The most important thing here we should all take home is that the works of the enemies shall not stand and if they persist, they shall go down for your sake. "Since thou are precious in my sight, thou hast been honourable, and I have loved thee: therefore, will I give men for thee, and people for thy life." Isaiah 43:4 (KJV).

You do not need further interpretation or explanation of this portion of the scripture. It is crystal clear that you are precious to Him and that He shall give nations as a ransom for your soul. It is your faith that will take you through. When you believe, then your miracles, signs, and wonders shall be complete. The Centurion believed and his faith healed his servant and Jesus did not go to his house to heal his servant. And he said, 'I am not worthy that Thou should come into my roof but say the word and my servant shall be healed.'

It is this faith that causes your mountains to be moved and cast into the bottomless sea. It is this faith that will cause your valley to become plain. It is this faith that will cause your crocked road to become straight.

It is this same faith that will set up your standard against your enemies when they come like a flood. It is this same faith that will cause your rocky roads to become plain and even tarred. It is this same faith that will make you walk through the sea and the water cannot overcome you. It is the same faith that will make you walk through the fire and the fire cannot consume you. Praise God!

It is this same faith that will cause you to sleep in the hungry lion's den and they guide and secure you through all day and night and even forever. He says that "He can do exceedingly, abundantly above your expectation or imagination according to the power that worked in you. What is the power, it is your belief system, faith, or mindset! Praise God! But now thus saith the LORD that created thee, O Jacob, and he that formed thee, O Israel, Fear not: for I have redeemed thee, I have called thee by thy name; thou art mine.

When thou pass through the waters, I will be with thee; and through the rivers, they shall not overflow thee: when thou walks through the fire, thou shalt not be burned; neither shall the flame kindle upon thee. For I am the LORD thy God, the Holy One of Israel, thy Saviour: I gave Egypt for thy ransom, Ethiopia and Seba for thee." Isaiah 43:1-3 (KJV).

The story of this man was pathetic until he encountered Christ the Lord. This man could not help himself. He used to live in the bushes, streets, and mountains and hurt himself with stones and other stuff. His relatives try to help but to no avail so much so that they bind him with chains, and he breaks through or loose.

His mind was taken over by those spirits and he could not know what he was doing and the same applies to many people today.

When he encountered the Holy and anointed One, his story changed, and the Lord also anointed us to serve His purpose on earth and even said that greater works shall we do. Praise God!

That is why such people usually have nightmares in their dreams. They often see themselves walking in the flood, in the bushes, and sometimes on bush paths. These people often find themselves walking in darkness, doing long walks, without end and missing their way in the dream. Being chased, and fighting even with masquerades, they see snakes and scorpions, cats, and dogs, losing money, dream deaths, near-miss accidents, offered poisonous food or drinks. These dreams are often repetitive or recurring. They see and deal with unknown spirits and sometimes with late relatives in their dreams. Whatever they set their hands to do will hardly work out. If you are in this group, please seek help. You cannot do it alone. There are men of God who are anointed to help.

That is why it is necessary to read and find out things for yourself. You must do it for yourself and no other person can do it for you. It is only you that will know and understand your predicament or what you are going through.

It is a man who did it to man. Sometimes, it may not be easy for people to understand what you are going through until revealed by God and you should learn to understand things by yourself through reading because the more you read, pray, and praise, the more the Lord will reveal Himself to you. Again, when you read, it will get you thinking about those things which you might have known and those you do not know.

"And God saw that the wickedness of man was great in the earth and that every imagination of the thoughts of his heart was only evil continually." Genesis 6:5 (KJV). That is what men are and we don't have to wait for God to tell us. He could be your brother, your brother-in-law, your wife or husband particularly when they have different agendas, your jealous friend, and so on. It must be somebody who knows you in your community particularly your father's friends whose children may not be doing as well and they say we will not allow him to reign over us.

However, in some cases, their children may be doing as well, but the evil in man to be an evil man will not allow them to leave you alone. The early you discover this, please seek help. Psalms 58:3 (KJV): "The wicked are estranged from the womb: they go astray as soon as they are born, speaking lies." If I may ask, are you living or have lived with a *lying,* deceitful, abusive, two-faced, or untruthful relative or a manipulator, if yes, then guess what the Bible is saying here.

These witches start their enterprise as soon as they are born. Most of them do not go for training. We will continue to pray for them, hopefully, the Lord will touch their spirit to change or repent. However, some are called by God and anointed by God to use the power or authority to do great and mighty things for the children of God, but they turn their power and use it for evil.

Even if they are from God and turn against you, it shall not stand nor shall it come to pass because He did not ask them to use them on you.

"Behold, they shall surely gather, but not by me: whosoever shall gather together against thee shall fall for thy sake. Behold, I have created the smith that bloweth the coals in the fire, and that bringeth forth an instrument for his work; and I have created the waster to destroy. No weapon that is formed against thee shall prosper; and every tongue that shall rise against thee in judgment thou shalt condemn. This is the heritage of the servants of the LORD, and their righteousness is of me, saith the LORD." Isaiah 54:15-17 (KJV).

It is not the desire of the wicked or what they have imagined doing that shall stand but the word of God. The word of God stands the test of time. It cannot fail without accomplishing the purpose for which it was sent, instead, let the heaven and the earth pass away.

When they use those weapons or witchcraft against you it shall not prosper because you are not born of flesh and blood but born of God. He ordained them to create and use the weapons, but He did not ask them to use them against you. If they try, it shall not work but fail because you are born of God and your righteousness is of Christ.

"And I will cut off the cities of thy land and throw down all thy strong holds: And I will cut off witchcrafts out of thine hand; and thou shalt have no more soothsayers": Micah 5:11-12 (KJV).

The Lord does not condone evil and those who practice it. It is not the desire of the wicked or that which they have imagined doing that shall stand but the will of God for you. The will of God and the word of God stands the test of time. It cannot fail without accomplishing the purpose for which it was sent, instead, let the heavens and the earth pass away.

"Let them shout for joy, and be glad, that favour my righteous cause: yea, let them say continually, Let the LORD be magnified, which hath pleasure in the prosperity of his servant." Psalm 35:27 (KJV).

Salvation is in the heart, and deliverance is in the mind. Even if you knowingly commit a sin and repent, you shall be forgiven. The Father has given us the kingdom, you can join as soon as you repent and are called sons of God.

When you join the fold, there will be no enchantment or divination against you that shall prosper. "Surely there is no enchantment against Jacob, neither is there any divination against Israel: According to this time it shall be said of Jacob and Israel, what hath God wrought!" Numbers 23:23(KJV). The Lord has done great and marvellous things for us and standing still with us for our deliverance and salvation. Praise Him!

Confession:
- I bind any strongholds in our lives and take them captive in the mighty name of Jesus.
- I decree and declare that any strongholds in our lives be brought down and destroyed in the Mighty name of Jesus.
- I decree and declare that any evil gathering against us shall catch the fire of the Holy Ghost by fire by force.
- I decree and declare that when they call our names for evil, heavenly thunder shall answer them with strike.
- The Bible says suffer not the witches to live, let them not see the light of the day.
- No weapon whatsoever that is fashioned against us shall prosper.
- Any tongue that rises against us in judgement shall be condemned.
- We go through the fire, it cannot consume us, and we go through the sea, the water cannot overcome us.
- No enchantment or divination against us shall prosper.
- The House of Jacob shall possess her possessions.
- Lord expose those who are causing pain in my life.
- Lord shame them so that they can confess with their mouth.
- As they plan evil, let it be to them like marrow in their bones.
- As they think and do evil, let not their evil depart from them and never touch the anointed ones and their families.

- Let their wickedness become shame and cover them in the mighty name of Jesus.
- Let not their evil depart from them and cover them with their shame in the mighty name of Jesus.
- Father, we thank You, we praise You oh Lord for You are the God of vengeance in Jesus' mighty name we pray, amen.
- In Jesus' Mighty name, we pray, Amen.

"My son, walk not thou in the way with them; refrain thy foot from their path": Proverbs 1:15 (KJV). *Please avoid the company of evil people because they are full of sickness, poverty, envy, jealousy, backbites and similar spirits including bareness.

2: Imaginations

Imagination is the ability to form a mental image of something that is neither seen nor perceived as real nor present to the senses. It is like having a vision of something in your mind or a mental picture of something which could be either positive or negative. Imagination is greater than knowledge, ideas, or understanding.

With knowledge, you can know a specific trade or profession. But with imagination, you can imagine the world at large or see the whole world in your mind even the heavens. Many artists use their imaginations to create things from abstracts. Apart from artists, many entrepreneurs and visionaries create many things from their imagination including products and services. Some of those imaginations become the words of your mouth.

They visualise an image or see with their mind's eye and design and create them. The ability to confront and deal with reality by using the creative power of the mind; and resourcefulness to gain victory over the enemies by believing and standing in the truth of God's word.

Imagination is so powerful so much that when a person thinks about a career, he is imagining and creating it in his mind. That is why when you ask a young person, what he would like to be and would answer you a doctor, lawyer, accountant, and so forth. You create your world through your thought system or mind and in the same vein or way, you can destroy any power or forces harassing your life. Your imagination creates your thoughts, desires, dreams, visions and spoken words because everything comes from the mind.

Witchcraft is an ideology that could be imagination or an illusion. It is a belief system or mindset. The African interpretation of witchcraft is that 'he is a black magic doctor who can afflict other people with evil and wicked spirit.'

On the other hand, the Cambridge English dictionary defines it as "the activity of performing magic to help or harm other people." These definitions are synonymous with each other. Affliction or harm is a mindset. If you believe that they can afflict or harm you, that is it but on the contrary, if you say they cannot, it shall not stand neither will they come to pass, then that is it for you. It is a belief system.

They can use witchcraft to hold someone back so that he does not achieve and at the same time, it can also be used to propel a person to success beyond belief. The difference is that only the Lord can make you prosper and be in good health without adding any sorrow to it.

Imagination is so powerful that you can imagine the whole world at a go, the past, present, and future. You can imagine how the Lord laid the beams of the earth in the seas, how it will look like when everywhere was covered with water and the earth was without form and void and darkness was on the face of the seas.

Imagine when the light appeared, and darkness gave way, and it could not comprehend it. Imagine the imagination of the Lord and how He formed the earth and all that is in it including the heavens. All are imaginations, can you imagine or comprehend the imagination? Imagine when there will be no more witchcraft, imagine when there will be no more pain, imagine when there will be no more sickness, imagine when there will be no more poverty, imagine when there will be no more barrenness, imagine when there will be no more death and all the evils on earth are completely wiped out. Imagine the imagination!

The heavens and the earth and the fullest thereof are the great imaginations of the Lord but all other things, products, and services are the imaginations of men because we are made in His image and likeness and born not of flesh or blood but of God.

Examples are shoes, dresses, bicycles, cars, trains, computers, webs, and aeroplanes to name but a few. Every creation of God and man is an image from the heart or mind, which became imagination, and turned into an idea and gets created or crystallised.

Everything was imagined including man and the Lord said, 'Let us make a man in our image, after our likeness,' and man was made. Imagination is a greater dream or vision because you can feel it and meditate on it even in your thinking, dreams, and visions.

"Before I formed thee in the belly I knew thee, and before thou camest forth out of the womb I sanctified thee, and I ordained thee a prophet unto the nations." Jeremiah 1:5 (KJV). You are holy, anointed, a masterpiece created, at such a time as this to perform great and mighty things for God, for the benefit of His people. Can you imagine it? You are fearfully and wonderfully made, and you know it. Praise God!

It is the truth that you knew that will make you free.

Ephesians 4:8 says, "Wherefore he saith when he ascended on high, he led captivity captive and gave gifts unto men." The Lord took all your enemies, captive before ascending to His Father. All those enemies are the witches, sickness, poverty, barrenness, sorrow, and even death that have been conquered. Many of us live with them because their minds or spiritual eyes are blinded, and they cannot see that they have been conquered. Instead, they see evil persisting when there is no evil.

The evils you are seeing are only in the mind because you are imagining them. Your life is in your mind, success or failure is in your mind or heart. Your battles in life are fought won or lost in your heart. Proverbs 11:27 says, "He that diligently seeketh good procureth favour: but he that seeketh mischief, it shall come unto him."

It is what you think or imagine that comes to you because they are in your mind as thoughts create. Crystallization of anything is a function of your mind, the way you think, reason, and do things including those around you and, the choices you make.

You take the captivities captive by not believing and thinking about them. Believe or have faith that the power of Jesus, which is in you is greater than the power in your enemies and that you have the authority to conquer, pull down, destroy and the power to plant and rebuild.

See it that you take authority in the blood of Jesus and condemn and bind all evils fashioned against you and your family even your friends and neighbours. If they do not want, you to succeed and want you to be:

- Sick – declare that you are healed by His stripes.
- Poor – declare that you are rich because He was made poor that we might be rich.
- Childless – declare that He had no children so that you might have them in abundance.
- Marriage – declare that He was a celebrity that you might marry.
- Stress – He went through the agony so that we might have a good life and have it more abundantly.
- Dead – declare that He died for me to live and live forever in an abundance of peace and prosperity.

The law of double jeopardy provides that a man cannot be punished twice for the same offence because He has taken the cross and cains even the death for us. Captivities have been taken captive. Most of the things we are going through and complaining about are from our imaginations because of the manipulation of our enemies.

Do not believe them nor think about them just cast them out and delete them each time they come to mind. It is not what they think about you, it is what you think about you. It is not what they say about you, it is what you declare about you. It is not what opinion they have about you, it is what you believe about yourself. It is a mindset or belief system.

The Bible made it clear that no weapon fashioned against us shall prosper. If you look at the Oxford University Dictionary's definition of witchcraft, it is the power to do good or harm someone.

It is anointing from God to do good, to bless, to heal, to anoint in righteousness, but the devil has led men to use them against God's children or otherwise. The Bible also confirms that the power is from God, but He did not give it to them to bewitch or harm you if they try it on the children of God, it shall not work and if they persist, they will go down for your sake.

"Since thou wast precious in my sight, thou hast been honourable, and I have loved thee: therefore, will I give men for thee, and people for thy life." Isaiah 43:4 (KJV).

The Lord can go to any length to protect us and fight for His children. Some of you might have seen the hen protecting the chicken from the kite or hawk or a lady protecting her baby.

Our Father goes beyond that and gives nations as a ransom for our lives. He gives your enemies as a ransom for your soul, only keep your hands and minds clean and believe in the faithful Almighty God. He went on to say that even if a breastfeeding mother forgets her baby, He will never forget us and will cause wickedness and evil people to go down for our sake.

"Can a woman forget her sucking child, that she should not have compassion on the son of her womb? yea, they may forget, yet will I not forget thee. Behold, I have gravened thee upon the palms of my hands; thy walls are continually before me.

Thy children shall make haste; thy destroyers and they that made thee waste shall go forth of thee." Isaiah 49:15-17(KJV). Thy destroyers shall be destroyed, and thy wasters shall be wasted because you are precious to Him.

"Behold, they shall surely gather, but not by me: whosoever shall gather together against thee shall fall for thy sake. Behold, I have created the smith that bloweth the coals in the fire, and that bringeth forth an instrument for his work; and I have created the waster to destroy. No weapon that is formed against thee shall prosper, and every tongue that shall rise against thee in judgment thou shalt condemn. This is the heritage of the servants of the LORD, and their righteousness is of me, saith the LORD." Isaiah 54:15-17 (KJV).

I had this lady who came with her husband asking for help because of witchcraft. She told me that they had been to this church and that church and saw these men of God without any luck. I told her that I have had the opportunity to minister a similar prayer to many other people, but the quick answer comes with your faith.

When the people of God pray and you believe that you have not been delivered and continue to think in the same manner, it will be difficult for you to be free or delivered. No matter what they hear in the churches each week, it does not make sense or difference to some of them. Jesus is a belief system, that is why he said to the lady with the blood issue, go in peace your faith has made you whole.

Salvation, healing, freedom, deliverance, and success are the functions of the mind. It is a mindset or belief system. You cannot have or get what you don't have or believe that you have received. "The centurion answered and said, Lord, I am not worthy that thou shouldest come under my roof: but speak the word only, and my servant shall be healed." Matthew 8:8 (KJV).

As I have already said it is a belief system. The faith in this military commander healed his servant and the Lord confessed that He had not seen such faith in Israel.

Your faith and little work will make the miracles. Some people will continue to remain in chains or bondages through unbelief, even though they have gone through their deliverance. It is like someone who left Egypt and had his mind fixed in Egypt which means that he is still there in bondage or house of exile. This is the power of imagination, as you continue to see those chains in your mind's eyes, you will continue to be in that bondage.

When you start imagining freedom and redemption in your heart, you will begin to see freedom even the chains shattered. You cannot see that the chains have been broken or witchcraft has been destroyed until you change your mindset.

"Keep thy heart with all diligence; For out of it are the issues of life." Proverbs 4:23 (KJV). Moving forward, backwards, or standing still is of the mind. You need to know what goes into your mind because it is the same thing that will be processed and come out of it.

If you sow fear, it will germinate, and you continue to be afraid of fear and fear any little thing. Fear is the spirit of negativity and is evil and not recommended by the scripture. Another important one is doubt which is lacking faith. If you believe and say to the mountain, be thou removed and cast into the sea, it shall be moved.

Your mind is likened to the computer's central processing unit. The computer will process any data entered and give you the answer, what the computer thinks is right and not what you presumed to be right.

Although your mind may discern between good and bad in some cases, you do not need to expose yourself to things that will lead you to think negatively or corrupt your mind. That is why you must guide it all diligence and not tempt yourself.

You must be very careful with what you think or imagine in your heart. The news you listen to, the books you read, the films you watch, and others that go through your sensory organs affect how you think and your imagination.

When you start thinking and imagining victory, success, greatness, and favour in your heart, that is what you will get, and you'll start walking in high places as they crystallise. But the moment you do the reverse, your life will change.

If you look carefully, most successful people are people who think in certain ways while others who think in other certain ways do not move on. All life issues revolve around and are resolved in the heart. All data concerning a person's life is processed there, in the heart and the result of it is what you become. It can face any life situation and resolve difficulties and resourcefulness.

We are made in the image and likeness of God and when He made heaven and the earth, He realised that the earth was without form and void. It was so because His imagination was not realised. He expected to see light and the light was not there.

He visualised the earth, He built a mental picture of it and when the light was missing, He stopped His creative work and called the light. It came forth and He said, 'This is good.' and He continued with His creative activities.

In Genesis 1: 26 He says, "Let us make man in our image and according to our likeness." You can see the vision and imagination there just as when He started thinking about creating heaven and the earth.

Most successful men are visionaries, they think ahead and plan strategically and at the same time manage their time very well because your life and how well you live will depend on how well you manage your life with the time available to you.

Successful men do not take no for an answer. When they are taking a thousand-mile journey, they know is going to be hard, but they think and plan for it. As soon as they take the first step, they don't stop until the end of the journey.

They knew that it would not be easy and everything in life is hard but one must choose his hardness and not quit. To quit means to fail and there's no failure in the dictionary of God. Therefore, you cannot fail. Praise God!

They have creative minds and see with the eyes of the mind of God. They do not give up when something does not work out fine once or twice. They believe and persevere until a solution is found. You cannot tell me that the best entrepreneurs, developers or athletes got it right the first time. A lot of work and effort was expended on their successes.

When you have a drawback or a setback, do not capitalise on it. Capitalise on your strength and look for corrective measures to keep things moving. Concentrate on your strengths. and improve more and avoid thinking and talking about your weaknesses or failures. By improving or focusing on your strength you are creating a niche or brand for yourself including packaging and pricing.

It is what you can offer, or the solution you provide that will bring you to the limelight and even before kings and great people will look for you. "A man's gift maketh room for him, and bringeth him before great men. He that is first in his cause seemeth just; but his neighbour cometh and searcheth him." Proverbs 18:16-17 (KJV).

Do not go on fighting unnecessary weakness in you but concentrate on your strength. When you show your talent, what you can do or offer, great people will look for you. Your brand or unique image becomes your identity. In this case, your talent becomes your identity. Praise God!

James 1:12 says, "Blessed is the man that endureth temptation: for when he is tried, he shall receive the crown of life, which the Lord hath promised to them that love him."

Yes, you must overcome obstacles in life to receive the crown of life which comes from God. We need that faith with some hard work to overcome because only the overcomers are crowned. Temptation can be any obstacle in one's life; we must overcome it to see the victory that will bring about the crown.

It's a man's gift that maketh room for him and bring him before kings. What can you put on the table? Wisdom, knowledge, understanding, product, service, technological breakthrough or what? Think about it and ask God why He brought you to this planet. If you do earnestly ask, He will reveal it to you. That is if He has not revealed it to you and you are unable to catch it.

Proverbs 6:6-8 says, "Go to the ant, thou sluggard; consider her ways, and be wise: Which having no guide, overseer, or ruler, provides her meat in the summer, and gathered her food in the harvest." The Lord made even the smallest animals think from their heart, to know that they will need food on a rainy day when the flood overtakes and destroys them if they come out.

As a result, they plan and put together all they will need during the rainy days until the summer days. It is all in the heart to plan strategically, stay still or go around the circle.

The ants do not need to be told; they plan out of their free mind. The Bible says as a man thinketh in his heart so is he. As you think, that is the faith that will need some work to be actualised. The expectation of the poor shall not perish forever. We must fulfil our heart desires in the mighty name of Jesus because the word of the Lord is yes and amen forever. His promises must come true.

Proverbs 24:16 says, "A just man falleth seven times, and riseth up again." The calling to greatness does not come easy. You need to work very hard. Do not give up and blame witches. If you work with God, He will guide you and tell you if there are some hands of the evil ones. Remember that the birth of Prophet Samuel did not come easy because he was going to be a great man neither did the birth of Isaac and John the Baptist. After all, they were very significant men, to mention a few.

Every significant man or thing goes through a process. Take the example of gold or silver, they are stones, though not found in common places, and at the same time, they go through rigorous processes to become what they are. Psalms 12:6. "The words of the LORD are pure words: as silver tried in a furnace of earth, purified seven times."

Everything must go through a process that may be difficult including production lines. It is so that the irrationality or foolishness and chaffs may be removed. The rubbished and the nonsenses must be cleared before they can be what the Lord wants them to be. Most men of God are very clean in nature and appearance because they have gone through this process of cleansing.

Gold is not found on the surface of the earth. You must dig deep to get it and notwithstanding the digging, it has to go through due process to become real or pure gold. The Lord prophesied the birth of the seed of the woman, and it did not come until about two thousand years ago. "Brethren, I count not myself to have apprehended: but this one thing I do, forgetting those things which are behind, and reaching forth unto those things which are before." Philippians 3:13 (KJV).

Apprehension means being in bondage, prison, caged, and without freedom. In other words, you can call it fear or the spirit of fear. The fear of fear can hold any person in bondage and sometimes kill. If you consider yourself apprehended, then you are bewitching yourself through fear of what happened in the past, or of the unknown.

We must renew our minds and think in a more positive manner believing that we have received whatever we are looking for or desire. Fear is not real; it is fantasy or imagination without knowing what the other person or opponent is thinking. He may even be more afraid of you without you knowing it.

You should stop thinking about that which stopped your father from succeeding in his education or business or of those who stopped your mother from having children on time or getting married. When you become a born-again Christian, stop thinking and speaking negatively about those evils that used to run in the family.

You may be surprised to know that with a positive mindset, He will restore unto you all the years His great armies such as the caterpillars, cankerworms and palmerworms have eaten in a billion folds (Job 2:25).

2 Corinthians 5:17 says, "Therefore, if any man is in Christ, he is a new creature: old things are passed away; behold, all things have become new." A new creature is one with a new heart, new mind, new mindset, new thinking and a different positive attitude and manner.

He sees life with different eyes and not as before, meaning that he has circumcised his heart. Forget about the past and forge new dreams. Do not hold yourself captive because this is just the time to hold your captivities captive. Go for the best things which are ahead or in front of you.

The Apostle Paul says he is reaching out for those things which are before and not the ones behind because if he went back from his life goals before the ministry and the pains, he suffered in the ministry he would not complete his course. Do not give in to any negative voices or pictures in your mind.

Concentrate on the positive side. Think positive, dream of success, speak greatness, sing victory for if Christ be for us who can be against us? Do not look at the pains, processes, and costs but focus on the price which is the gold.

This name and the blood take all captivities captive. If anything did not go well or quickly the way you would want it, then do some fasting. If you need help or someone to join you to agree with you in prayer, you can get your pastor or anybody who has the same spirit as you or give me a call to join you and agree with you for we are all **one** in the body of Christ. Mark 9:29 says, "And he said unto them, this kind can come forth by nothing but by prayer and fasting."

For Christ is in us, we have the power to command the mountains to move and they shall obey, and if they refuse, we have no alternative but to take it by force and do it by fasting and prayer. The result is that they must obey the Word of God because all powers and principalities are the product of the Word of God, and they must hear the Word of God.

The Bible says, 'At the mention of the name of Jesus, every knee shall bow and all tongues shall confess that He is Lord.' (Philippians 2:10-11). He will do exceedingly abundantly above your imagination depending on the power that worketh in you.

The power in you will depend on your ability to absorb the Word of God which is your faith. Faith cometh by hearing and hearing by the Word of God.

Faith is your belief system, and you cannot get or go beyond your level of faith. It is that truth you know that will make you free and that truth is what you believe to be true, and it is a mindset. When you walk on high anointing every yoke shall be destroyed because the Bible says, 'The yoke is destroyed because of the anointing.' (Isaiah 10:27).

Then you walk from favour to favour, from glory to glory, from superabundance to superabundance, from peace to peace, from joy to joy, and grace to grace because the yoke is destroyed because of the power of the anointing and that is your victory. That anointing is the grace with which the pastors are using to pray for healing and casting out demons.

Your imagination, thoughts, mind, and heart must be geared towards victory, success, triumph, and greatness to be able to walk in high places. Those thoughts, imaginations, and visualizations create your future. Therefore, do not be on the negative of them instead, always be on the positive.

A negative person or thinker will be held back because of his attitude and utterances, and he will be blaming witches when in real terms the witchcraft is him and he is blaming others. When a person fails to understand where their problems are coming from, he will, as a result, continue to bind and lose the wrong strongholds.

He may be the cause of the problems without knowing it. It is therefore imperative that we check ourselves very well to identify where the problems are coming from. The problem identified is half solved. Without knowing who the enemy is, it will not be possible for us to shoot our arrows or bullets which are the Word of God accurately. A lot of time is wasted aiming at the wrong targets, and one may perhaps shoot his foot.

You might be responsible for your challenges because of the way you think and speak, the choices you make, and the companions you keep. The way you think and speak will determine how far and quickly your breakthrough will come because the Bible says as a man thinketh in his heart so is he.

The companies or friends you keep will also affect your life positively or adversely particularly what they say or do. If you are a king, you must think and speak about reigning by declaring:

- I AM BORN TO REIGN!

If you are an over-comer, keep declaring it and do not stop it:
- I AM AN OVER-COMER,
- I OVERCOME THEM WITH THE BLOOD OF JESUS AND THE WORDS OF MY TESTIMONIES!

If you are looking for victory declare:
- I AM VICTORIOUS,
- I AM THE WINNER,
- I AM A VICTOR,
- I AM MORE THAN A CONQUEROR!

If you are looking for blessings of any kind, you confess:
- I AM HIGHLY BLESSED AND FAVOURED,
- ALL NATIONS SHALL CALL ME BLESSED,
- BLESSING SHALL CALL ME BLESSED,
- I AM FULL OF GRACE!

It is Faith and Word that move mountains and not self-pity. Those things which are not, you declare them as they were, or you have received them.

The Bible says decree a thing and it is be established unto thee. When this grace is established in your life, every yoke is destroyed, and you'll keep walking and dwelling in victory because it is in the mind, and you have favour with God and with men because you are born of God and not of the flesh and blood.

You have victory. Where others failed to receive, you shall receive because you are carrying His divine favour and living in His divine nature.

Psalm 24:9 says, 'Lift your heads, O ye gates; even lift them, ye everlasting doors; and the King of glory shall come in.' When you invite the King of Glory into your life, He will come in. He is looking for those who are thirsty for Him.

He does not go where He is not wanted. As He is in you and dwells in you, you will be witnessing remarkable changes in your life, thus moving from the ordinary to the extraordinary. You will no longer be the same.

He comes in the form of favour, blessings, success, victory, grace, or abundant life. Favour will come to you when you call favour and walk in favour and speak and walk in grace.

Success, victory, and abundant life come when you imagine or have the image of them in your mind and speak of them. They go to those who call them to come into their lives because they are part of the King of Glory who is the Christ in you.

You speak and meditate them day and night and as soon as they are released by the Lord from heaven, they look for you because your name is changed in the spiritual realm to favour, grace, victory, success, anointed, glory, joy, peace, abundance and so on.

They are new every day and are released by the Lord daily to locate you and rest on you.

"Behold, I stand at the door and knock: if any man hears my voice, and opens the door, I will come into him and will sup with him, and he with me. To him that overcomes will I grant to sit with me on my throne, even as I also overcame, and am set down with my Father in his throne. Revelation 3:20-21 (KJV).

The Lord is that Love which you are looking for, He is that Peace you are looking for, He is that abundance which you are looking for, He is that Success which you are looking for, He is that fruitfulness which you are looking for. He is an embedment of all the good things you have been looking for.

He is everything wonderful and marvellous, just invite Him into your life and try Him and see His miracles in you. He even promised you a sit in His Father's kingdom if you can overcome. He was tempted and found fit to sit at the right hand of the Father because He overcame the world even for us.

We are also expected to overcome to be able to be like him on earth and in heaven. He wouldn't be there if He did not overcome death and perhaps, we wouldn't be Christians today if He did not achieve those successes.

He has already stated that 'it is the Father's good pleasure to give us the kingdom.' The blessing starts from here on earth when you obey and walk in His status - that is to say 'believe in your own beliefs. You must be positive and in line with the Son of Man. Numbers 14:28 says, "Say unto them, As truly as I live, saith the LORD, as ye have spoken in mine ears, so will I do to you: Your carcasses shall fall in this wilderness."

When you call your ashes beauty, so they shall be but when you think and declare negativity the Lord will also agree with you.

This world is spirit and is a mind game. All the battles and games are played in the mind, attitude, and mental toughness.

When the children of Israel professed that they would not enter the promised land, the Lord agreed with them and only those who believed that they would make it - Joshua and Celeb made it. Only imagine, stand, and declare those truths which will make you free.

"For if the trumpet gives an uncertain sound, who shall prepare himself for the battle?" I Corinthians 14:8 (KJV). The Holy Spirit is, of course, aware of your situation and the Word of God requires you to speak out whatever is your need or heart's desire.

The Ministerial angels specially assigned to assist you are waiting for your instructions, but when the trumpet is unclear no one will be ready to go to battle for you. You must be specific in your petition to God through your prayers and you will see that the heavens will open their windows and fight your course.

"For God is not the author of confusion, but peace, as in all churches of the saints." I Corinthians 14:33 (KJV). Anything you desire, to do or have, you must believe that you already have them. Imagine it in your heart that you have received them and there is no way you can receive anything in the physical without believing in your heart that you have already received them.

You must believe them to be true before you even begin to confess them with your mouth. There is no way you can receive what you do not believe in your heart and see it to be true. You cannot pray unless you have conceived it in your heart because everything comes from the heart.

"Be careful of nothing, but in everything by prayer and supplication with thanksgiving let your request be made known unto God." Philippians 4:6 (KJV).

The Word of God here tells us to be careful of nothing, meaning that you should not fear anything but put everything in prayer to God boldly and believe that you have received the answers without wavering or doubting in your minds. You can learn from the Canaanite woman who refused to give in to the bluff of our Lord Jesus. When the Lord refused to give her a favourable answer she went, "Yes You are right, Lord," she said. "Even the dogs can eat from the crumbs that fell from their master's table." Matthew 15:27.

At that moment, the Lord immediately attended to her. It is your faith and your ability to maximise the truth in the Word of God. You have everything and everything is in you. Nobody can take it from you unless you give it to them for nothing or out of ignorance.

The Lord says, "No man taketh it from me, but I lay it down of myself. I have the power to lay it down, and I have the power to take it again. This commandment have I received of my Father." John 10:18 (KJV).

Nobody, power, or principality has power over my life unless I lay it down for them. Of course, I cannot give it to them because we are justified, sanctified, and covered with the blood of Jesus.

No weapon whatsoever that is fashioned against us shall prosper and any tongue that rises against us in judgement shall not prosper but condemned and that is our heritage as the sons of God and our righteousness is of Christ and not of our own or merited. To us who received Him and believed in Him, we have power and are declared the sons of God and that is our heritage. His righteousness is in us.

And the Lord said, "Behold, the people are one, and they have all one language; and this they begin to do: and now nothing will be restrained from them, which they have imagined doing." Genesis 11:6 (KJV). Here the Lord came down and saw the tower which the people were building because they were one and He stopped them by confusing them through many languages.

The Lord said to His Son "See the people are one and they speak one language and if they imagine doing anything, no one can stop them." The same thing applies to us because a house that is divided cannot stand. Therefore, you must believe in your heart and confess with your tongue that Jesus is Lord. Your spirit, body, and soul must agree with your belief system, and you will find out that you are unmovable. You must be determined and decisive in whatever you believe and think about actualising them.

Avoid doubts and double minds, Revelation 3:16 says, "So then, because you are lukewarm, and neither cold nor hot, I will vomit you out of My mouth." This means that this person does not know what he/she is doing or wants. He will vomit him. This goes on to say he may not succeed until he is sure of what he wants. It is the Spirit that moves, and you have to have the right Spirit in your mind to move actively, decisively, and effectively in your life.

It is all about you and not what your enemies are thinking or doing about you because a curse cannot curse the curse-less.

If you and your spouse or relative or pastor can speak one language nothing can stop your victory for the Word of God says that where two shall agree as touching anything they shall ask they shall receive.

"Again, I say unto you, that if two of you shall agree on earth as touching anything that they shall ask, it shall be done for them of my Father which is in heaven." Matthew 18:19. If the Lord says He cannot stop you then no person, power, or principality can stop you except your imagination, thinking and utterances.

The greatest device of the enemies is to use your spouse to disagree with you and fight you so that there will be no agreement. The apostles prayed in one accord and the Holy Ghost came down. When a family speaks one language, works in one accord, and prays together, I tell you the truth, nothing can hinder them. If you believe you are fighting a just course with a clear vision, call me and I will agree with you in prayer.

The Bible says, 'The prayer of the righteous availeth much.' Praise God!

Make this declaration:

- I have overcome the world with the precious blood of Jesus and the word of my testimonies.
- I am a victorious one.
- I am more than a conqueror.
- I can do all things through Christ who strengthens me.
- I am born to reign even forever in Jesus' mighty name, Amen!
- Hallelujah, Praise God!

As you pray, you must imagine them to be true in your heart.

3: Casting Down Imaginations

Imagination is a mental image or pictures, dreams, or visions which could be negative or positive. It is the faculty or action of forming new ideas and creativity. Now let's consider what the Word of God says concerning us on the positive side.

Genesis 1:28 says, "And God blessed them, and God said unto them be fruitful, and multiply, and replenish the earth, and subdue it: and have dominion over the fish of the sea, and over the fowl of the air, and over every living thing that moves upon the earth."

Here the Lord pronounced blessings upon His children and asked us to multiply, increase and fill the earth and have dominion or reign over all the earth.

The Lord was at that time, seeing increases and multiplications in our lives in His mental pictures, mental images, or imaginations. He was seeing those things which were not as they were or existed or created in His mind's eyes or spiritual eyes.

It is the ability to see with spiritual eyes or form a mental image of something that is not present or perceived as they were or had been. He also asked us to take authority over everything He had created.

"Being justified freely by His grace through the redemption that is in Christ Jesus: Whom God hath set forth to be a propitiation through faith in his blood, to declare his righteousness for the remission of sins that are past, through the forbearance of God." Romans 3:24-25 (KJV).

We are now justified, sanctified, reconciled, and set apart for the Lord through the blood of our Lord Jesus Christ through faith. In this wise, the blessing pronounced by God in the garden of Eden still stands for those who love the Lord and who are called according to His purpose.

Papa Adam did not do anything to merit it and the same with Daddy Abraham. Neither do we need to do anything except to receive Jesus Christ as our Lord and personal savior.

It is free for those who believe in His Son Jesus Christ because He has given us the power to become sons of God. Through Him and the shading of His blood to repurchase us.

All creatures have the original blessing of the Father, but it is only those who believe in it with a certain mindset that keeps it.

To get anything you must create it in your mind and believe it to be true before it comes to be, including education, family, business, and whatever it may be. Nothing extraordinary is required but belief. That does not mean that you will not encounter any obstacles.

On the stem or branch of a rose flower, are thorns that you must pass through before getting to the flower. It is the same in all situations, everyone must go through the process. Provided you do not quit or crash on the way, your success is assured.

"For I know the thoughts that I think toward you, saith the LORD, thoughts of peace, and not of evil, to give you an expected end." Jeremiah 29:11(KJV). The Father desires that you prosper and be in peace and good health. To have a good life with nothing missing or broken.

You will look back and see the goodness of the Lord in your life and family. That same blessing as in the garden of Eden and to

Abraham. He has always blessed His people and expects us to live and walk in His glory.

In John 10:10 Our Lord talked about bringing to us abundant life. Talking about imagination and the promises or blessings of God, why are some people getting these blessings while others are not receiving them?

Papa Adam was blessed because the Lord made everything available including gold and other precious stones in the Garden of Eden before locating him there. Besides, He had a direct blessing from God before the serpent tempted him.

The sin although brought death, did not stop him from living what can be seen today as a reasonable and abundant life. I pray that the Lord will prepare your blessings in your location and help you to locate them. Amen.

Many generations of the descendants of Papa Adam were blessed and that was based on their mindsets. When you look at the story of Cain and Abel, you see that Cain killed his brother following the acceptance of the offering of his brother and he became jealous and killed him.

What caused the problem, was their mindsets. Abel was bent on giving the best to his Father and Creator while his brother had a different spirit, the Lord accepted his brother's offering which resulted in the Lord rejecting his offering and he became angry and killed his brother.

Before the offerings were made, both of them had thoughts in their minds about what to give and how to go about them. Acceptance or rejection of their offerings by God was decided by God when He saw what was in their hearts. You cannot have good in your heart and give bad, neither can you have bad and give good. Look at the law of cause and effect.

The cause is the imagination in our heart which is purely spiritual, and the effect is the manifestation or answer in the natural which is also spiritual. The thoughts, imaginations, or mental pictures of Abel might have been to give the Lord, his best so that the Lord would be pleased and that is exactly what he did while his brother had a different spirit. You cannot sow the best and reap the less. Whatsoever a man sows, that he shall reap.

If a man sow blessing which is a life without lack, pain, sickness, sorrow, or even death for He hath conquered death for us. Similarly, Apostle John in his letter in 3 John 2 says, "Above all thing that we are in good health and prosper as our soul prospered." Prosperity does not necessarily mean financial prosperity alone but all the round sound mind and good health and nothing missing or broken.

A life in which one can look back and give glory to the Father who is art in heaven. Such a good life can only be imagined and created in the heart before manifestation in the physical. "There shall nothing cast their young, nor be barren, in thy land: the number of thy days I will fulfil." Exodus 23:26 (KJV).

You can have a more fulfilling life by imagining and applying the word of the Lord which says, "Whosoever that believes in me shall never die and if he has died shall come back to life."

It is what you choose to believe that you will imagine and meditate upon and that to your reality. "Jesus said unto her, I am the resurrection, and the life: he that believeth in me, though he were dead, yet shall he live: And whosoever lives and believeth in me shall never die. Believest thou this"? John 11:25-26 (KJV).

The blessing of God to Papa Adam, the thought of peace and the expected end of man in the book of Jeremiah, abundant life in the book of John, and prosperity mean the same thing.

They have already been done for us, and they are in us except that many of us are very busy imagining lack, poverty, sickness, and even death, and that is why these things are prevalent in the world today. Your life is created in your mind and your imagination determines how far you can go in life.

These are the promises of God, and the Word of God is to us yes and amen to the glory of the Father. "For all the promises of God in him are yea, and in him Amen, unto the glory of God by us." 2 Corinthians 1:20 (KJV). Some of these blessings do not come true because of the way some people think and talk. The Lord says, 'What you say I will do.' Numbers 14:28.

There is also no way a man can get what he does not know or believe in. Even if you get what you do not know, it may not make sense to you because you may not care to learn or know what to do with it. Therefore, you may not get the full benefit of it because you do not know it's worth or value.

Everything we do or do not comes from the heart. For every action, there must be a reaction and it is much easier to get a negative reaction than a positive reaction. For example, when the Lord created the earth darkness came before the Lord called light to overtake it.

Therefore, we must be very careful as to what we think and speak. Now listen to the prayer of the Psalmist which says, "Let the words of my mouth, and the meditation of my heart, be acceptable in thy sight, O LORD, my strength, and my redeemer." Psalm 19:14.

The word of your mouth is from the abundance of your heart which is your meditation, imagination, thought system, and intuition or clairvoyance. That is why we need to think great and big to be able to succeed in life.

It is wicked to be negative not only to yourself but to others too because we are all linked together by His Spirit. And the Lord sees the heart of man, even before the man can do that which he has imagined. As we are all linked up through Him, whatever we desire for others shall also come to you.

"And God saw that the wickedness of man was great in the earth and that every imagination of the thoughts of his heart was only evil continually." Genesis 6:5 (KJV).

Genesis 5:23-24 says, "And all the days of Enoch were three hundred sixty and five years: And Enoch walked with God: and he was not; for God took him." Can you see the spirit of this man? His imagination was to do good and walk with the Father and he did, and the Lord took him to be with Him without tasting death, where he can walk side by side with Him.

Look again at His son who had a different mindset of abundant life on earth and the Lord granted him his heart's desire. Genesis 5:27 says, "And all the days of Methuselah were nine hundred sixty and nine years: and he died."

It is where your treasure is that your mind will be. You get whatever you sow in your mind through your imagination. "For where your treasure is, there will your heart be also." Matthew 6:21 (KJV).

A man who is afraid of death and as a result thinks about death is more likely to die than a man who is busy with his work and does not remember death. The more you think about peace, you get peace, love, you get love, and then success you see success. We create and attract anything we imagine in our hearts.

Proverbs 21:18 says, 'As a man thinketh in his heart so is he.' Often people hold themselves back through their imaginations and blame them on the witches. When a person is imagining negativity and his life is turning upside down, it is he who is bewitching himself and no other person.

Of course, negativity is witchcraft and must be cast down. "For though we walk in the flesh, we do not war after the flesh: (For the weapons of our warfare are not carnal, but mighty through God to the pulling down of strongholds;) Casting down imaginations, and every high thing that exalted itself against the knowledge of God and bring into captivity every thought to the obedience of Christ." II Corinthians 10:3-15 (KJV).

The bondage, limitation, or stronghold are the attitudes we display based on our thought systems. The Lord said in blessing, I have blessed you, in multiplication, I have multiplied you. If you cannot believe and accept the blessing and multiplication, how can you be blessed and multiply?

When you do not believe and keep doing your best to break through, you are very unlikely to break through because the stronghold in you, need to be broken before you can forge ahead. You cannot make a budget and achieve it without believing in it.

Your life, which is the real you are in your mind and your thought system. You are your inner man and not the flesh and blood which you are seeing and feeling. That is where you create and recreate yourself. That is where you plan and manage your life.

Your success, promotion, and acceleration and how far you can go will all depend on your thinking and the choices you make. The imagination of fears, doubts, and any other that might lead you to doubt the power and grace of God in you must be cast out and brought to the obedience of Christ the King.

He told you; I have blessed you; I have multiplied you, and from your seed shall all the nations of the earth be blessed. Believe Him and thank Him for the blessing, imagine and meditate upon it and it shall come upon you and overtake you wherever you are.

There is a young medical doctor in Ireland working on a contract or temporary basis and his work was very irregular subjecting the family to suffering in meeting their bills and other daily needs. His wife asked for prayer knowing that this class of people is sought after and why is their own different.

After the prayer and a while, the lady called back to thank God for a prayer well answered. Anything exalting itself against your destiny must be brought down to the obedience of Christ. It does not matter if it is your mind, thought system, or witchcraft, they must be brought down to the obedience of Christ the King.

There are different types of people, those who believe that they can do it – that is the 'I cans', those who like to postpone what they can do today for tomorrow, and those who think that they 'can't be able.'

Those who keep the work for tomorrow will find out that there are other things for that day, and they become too much for that day and they push them further to the next day and not getting anything done for the week, month, or even for the year. How do you think these people can make headway in life?

Coming to the 'I can't' people are always afraid where there is no fear. They are always afraid of everything and full of doubts in their minds. They cannot do anything and that in turn turns to laziness. Their imagination or thinking is usually of 'it is difficult, it is hard.'

Everything is hard or difficult when you think that way, but they are not hard and can be enjoyable and easy when you set your mind to appreciate the gift of God because it is He who gave you the power to create wealth. Other people are looking for the same opportunity.

The 'I cans' are the focused and determined people who are destined to succeed in life. They are destined to win and have victory and would not take no for an answer. When they see an opportunity, they don't waste time taking advantage of it. They don't stop because it could be a lifetime opportunity. They wouldn't keep what they could do and finish today for tomorrow.

They have their diary full and follow it step by step and tick off any completed assignments. The Bible says, 'whatsoever your hand finds to do, do it with your whole heart as if you are doing it to the Lord.' They take anything seriously and to the best of their ability.

They have goals for every dream and vision. When you do anything for God, you must do it well because you are doing it for yourself and your family and humanity. There is always a cause and effect for everyone for whatever you do or fail to do.

Although we live on the earth, our struggle is not physical or after the flesh, it is against powers and principalities, against the rulers of this dark world, and spiritual wickedness in high places. One important point here to take home is that the battles we face here on earth are never carnal or physical irrespective of the form they appear.

You see a brother fighting his brother, father against son, and daughter against mother to name just a few. Sometimes, when asked about the issue, they cannot explain, and you find out that there is nothing behind it but there is something or reason behind it because they are spiritual.

Those who are not spiritually discerned cannot see it or understand it. The world is spiritual, and everything emanates from the spirit before manifesting in the physical. We must find their sources and foundation and uproot and pull them off the ground. They are powers and principalities and must be rooted out using the amours of God which is in Christ Jesus because we are born of God.

Revelation 10:12 refers to him as 'The great dragon and the old serpent.' A dragon is a very powerful beast that does not give up easily and fights to the end. However, he is a failure because his greatest mistake was to allow Christ to be crucified. The victory by Christ over death and sin rendered them powerless and hopeless because sin and death were their strength.

Stronghold is unbelief and believing in anything that can hold you back. A stronghold is a prison or bound in a chain. Many of us read and write about the bondage of the children of Israel in Egypt but we do not appreciate the meaning of the concept.

Bondage is when one is in prison or another person's slave as the children of Israel were in Egypt. That is what we know to be in bondage, but the actual bondage is in the heart of your mind. When you begin to think about those impossibilities and say 'I cannot, I am not able, it's too much. Stop! Stop!!

For with God, nothing shall be impossible because He's the God of no impossibilities and we are His children made in His image and likeness therefore nothing shall be impossible for us. We are for signs and wonders. If you believe say 'amen.'

The other night it was just terrible for me, and I prayed all night and found myself on top of the world (in the cloud) and I enquired what this meant. I remember that the Lord spoke to me and said, "A good son maketh a glad Father and a foolish son is the heaviness of his mother."

This means that we have all things and do not know how to manage them and that is why so many people are sick and poor on this earth which is full of potential, resources, and superabundance. A lot of people go to bed empty tummy in a world full of abundance for lack of knowledge. To know a little about the abundance on earth, some politicians will loot so much that they would not know what to do with the loot and cannot even create jobs for the hungry masses.

Bondage is in the mind because when you cannot think or reason properly, it can be said that you are under a spell or bondage like any other mad person or someone with an unsound mind.

How can a normal man live in abundance and be poor? Think of it! Poverty is the greatest bondage because of foolishness. That is why the Lord cried out and said, 'My people are destroyed for lack of knowledge.'

Your dreams, aspirations, and visions must be very clear for you to carry them through because where there is no vision the people perish or have the vision without clarity. You cannot take off on a journey without knowing where you are going. You must have a bus stop or destination.

A spirit of 'fear, cannot, or impossibility' must be cast down or out immediately. We do not need them anywhere near us. The serpent is a very wise and subtle animal and uses his cunning or craftiness to deceive Adam in the Garden of Eden. He is the same today. He can enter your mind to tell you more lies.

If he cannot get you, he will start with new lies. If he cannot directly get you, he can turn to your spouse, friends, or other relatives. Do not, I repeat, do not believe him. Negative imaginations are from the serpent and the devil and are unacceptable.

There is no stronghold except in the heart. It is a belief system that is holding a man from thinking right and moving forward. A good thinker should have a mindset or mental attitude to move him and his community forward. The stronghold is believing in those negative things which cannot move you forward but hold you captive and in prison. Stronghold is lies, false, and does not exist except in your heart or imagination. Anything which can hold you against the will of God for you or exalt itself against the knowledge of God must be or come from your heart. They must be erased and deleted to enable you to renew your mind and form the great and right mental attitude to possess your possessions.

Do not believe him or think about them. When such imaginations come into your mind, rebuke them, and return them to the senders with fire and brimstone because he is the father of all liars. They are not yours in Jesus' name. Amen.

When you begin to see those negative images or hear negative voices that your mother and your elder sisters did not get married and so you won't. Your father, uncles, and brothers could not make it in their careers, business, ministry, or family, rebuke those imaginations and cast them out because it is the enemies that are putting those in your mind. If you continue to listen and meditate on them, you might be lured to believe them.

Now think about King David who was the least in his father's house and the Lord chose him and made him the greatest King of Israel and ignored his big brothers. Think about brother Jabez whose mother gave the name and he cried to the Lord and the Lord blessed him and he became a new creature. 1 Chronicles 4:9-10.

He can do exceeding, abundantly, and above what we can expect or imagine and that's why He is God working with your faith or belief system.

Some people think they cannot go to university or do certain things because it is a privilege for a certain class of people. Perhaps their father and other elderly ones in the family could not do them. Education is no more a privilege but a right of any child.

If there is any barrier in the family, any person can break it, irrespective of the person's position in the family. When God asked Prophet Samuel to go to the house of Jesse to anoint the second King of Israel, He did not tell him to go for the first or second sons but for David who was the least in the family.

The issue here is positioning your mind to receive because the Lord looks at the heart before anointing a person. David was resolute in his ability to secure his sheep amid lions and other wild animals. "Thy servant slew both the lion and the bear: and this uncircumcised Philistine shall be as one of them, seeing he hath defied the armies of the living God." 1 Samuel 17:36 (KJV). Your stature does not define you or matter but how you position yourself in your mind.

That same God can also use you irrespective of your colour, place of birth, height, standing in the family or community, or education. The Lord can do the same for you if you walk in faith without wavering. Abraham believed in the Word of God and walked in it, and it was credited to him for righteousness (Romans 4:3).

Some people have already concluded that they cannot make it in their life and that is the biggest witchcraft because they have chosen their bus stop. How can God help you when you do not want to help yourself, be helped or believe in hope? Anything contrary or against the will of God must be brought down or cast out because they are all in the heart.

Your success is in your determination to succeed. It is your focus, and to look ahead strategically in the hope of success and achievement. The anticipation of your heart desires will get your spirit man or subconscious mind to create them for you and ensure that the results are achieved. The Lord will work for you when you believe that you can do it because it is impossible to please God without faith and He is a great rewarder for those that put their trust in Him.

They look back and see that their father failed, and their uncle tried and failed too. They looked at their family tree and found that their grandfather could not make it while he was alive, and their great-grandfather was the same story.

History cannot continue to repeat itself when the Spirit of God is in your life and that of your family. But without faith it is impossible to please him: for he that cometh to God must believe that he is and that he is a rewarder of them that diligently seek him. Hebrews 11:6 (KJV).

What you need to do is change your mindset or thought system, otherwise, you will end up with the same result. All imaginations and thoughts that try to exalt themselves above the knowledge of the Word of God should be brought into captivity and the obedience of Christ, a name above all names.

Casting down imaginations and thoughts means that you must, first, reject any negativity in your mind, and rebuke the spirit that is responsible for such negative ideas because you are born to effect a change. It's the set time to favour Zion.

Many evil men prosper and live long because they have set their mindset or imagination to live long and that nothing can stop them. They believe that they can get away with their evils without being caught.

They get caught sometimes after a while because they are breaching the law of the spirit which is the law of nature. Wickedness and evil are abominations in the spirit and natural world which is why they are caught sometimes. If they use that mindset rightly, there may be no limits to what some of them can do without evil thoughts.

If the foundation is not good, the building cannot hold. Psalm 11:3 says, "If the foundations are destroyed, what can the righteous do?" Do not mock yourself, for whatsoever a man sows, so he shall reap. Imagine true faith, true righteousness, true prosperity, and success and they shall be established for you. Blessed are the merciful for they shall see mercy because they sowed it.

James 4:7 says, "Draw close to God and oppose the devil and he shall flee from you." When you reject those negative thoughts and imaginations and return them to the sender with fire and thunder a few times, the sender will stop sending them to you because they can see that you are rejecting them even to their detriment.

The old serpent knows that if he can work through your mind, then he will overcome you. He cannot overcome you in the name of Jesus because greater is He that is in you than he that is in the world. It is the mind that controls the behaviour of the man.

The man's attitude to life will always come from his mind. A man who talks well and behaves well has a good mindset for from out of the abundance in the heart the mouth speaks. A man cannot give what he has not, you always give what you have.

Cast down the thoughts or imaginations that your uncle, mother-in-law, or sister-in-law is bewitching you. Always cover yourself, your family, business, and substances with the blood of Jesus and declare that 'No weapons whatsoever that is fashioned against you, your family, business or other substances shall prosper, for that is your heritage as the son of God and your righteousness is not of you but of Christ.'

Ye are of God, little children, and have overcome them: because greater is he that is in you than he that is in the world. 1 John 4:4 (KJV).

Always speak the truth and you must declare them aloud:

- I am the most blessed.
- I am blessed in the city; I am blessed in the field.
- My goings and comings are blessed.
- Blessed are the fruits of my body and the fruits of my ground.

- I am the righteousness of God.
- I am blessed beyond curses and witchcraft.
- I can do all things through Christ who strengthens me!

Imagine these words of truth and keep speaking them day and night. They should not depart from your mouth because they are Spirit and are Life.

"It is the spirit that quickened; the flesh profited nothing: the words that I speak unto you, they are spirit, and they are life" (John 6:63).

A man's mind plans his way: but the Lord directs his steps and makes them sure." Proverbs 16:9 (AMP). It is the mind that determines your direction because the Lord has given you that free mind to make decisions for yourself. If you walk in His counsel, then He will direct your steps and you cannot walk in darkness for His light will always guide you through.

"For to be carnally minded is death, but to be spiritually minded is life and peace." Roman 8:6 (KJV).

A carnally minded person is somebody who is walking in the flesh. He sees things as they appear in the physical world and does not believe that he can ask that hill to move, and it will move. He does not understand or see spiritual things.

He is moved by what he hears or sees around him and how he feels. His mind is set on carnal things which do not conform to the Word of God and often lead to death. Do not accept any nonsense in your heart. Neither should you allow them into your mind. Delete any nonsense thoughts and dreams. If they recur or persist, you delete and pray over them.

Whereas a spiritual-minded person walks by faith and not by sight. He is not often bothered when he sees the giants, roundabout him because he knows that the Lord is with him, and nothing can shake him (For we walk by faith, not by sight:) 2 Corinthians 5:7 (KJV).

If the Lord be for you, who can be against you? Nobody can stand in your way. Enemies, powers, and principalities will see that you are called by the name of the Lord Jesus Christ, and they will flee. You need to have the mindset of God, which is of boldness and sound mind, in His Word so that you may have life and have it more abundantly.

"And when the servant of the man of God was risen early, and gone forth, behold, a host compassed the city both with horses and chariots. And his servant said unto him, Alas, my master! how shall we do?

And he answered Fear not: for they that be with us are more than they that be with them. And Elisha prayed, and said, LORD, I pray thee, open his eyes, that he may see. And the LORD opened the eyes of the young man, and he saw: and behold, the mountain was full of horses and chariots of fire round about Elisha" 2 Kings 6:15-17 (KJV).

I pray the Lord to open your mind's eyes so that you can see that nothing shall be impossible and those who are with us are much more than those against us.

It is the word of faith that should be your belief system. Whatsoever you believe to be true, becomes truth in your life. Therefore, be very careful of what you read, listen to, or watch particularly on television and movies.

Your heart is the engine that drives your life, therefore be very careful of your thoughts and imaginations before they begin to create realities of your life that could be either negative or positive. Many people cannot get a miracle because of their mindsets. The Lord, Jesus could not perform many miracles in Galilee because of their mindset of Him.

There is no way, you can get a miracle when you do not believe in it. You can only get what you want because as you believe in those miracles which you are looking for, they will also be looking for you. Clear law of attraction.

"And when Jesus departed thence, two blind men followed him, crying, and saying, thou son of David, have mercy on us. And when he has come into the house, the blind men came to him: and Jesus saith unto them, Believe ye that I can do this? They said unto him, Yea, Lord. Then touched he their eyes, saying, according to your faith be it unto you. And their eyes were opened; and Jesus straitly charged them, saying, see that no man know it." Matthew 9:27-30 (KJV).

One important piece of advice here is that we should learn to keep certain things to ourselves even our miracles. Sometimes we dream of miracles and go forth to tell people who do not want us to have them, and they help us to lose them, even out of excitement. You don't tell everything to every person. Learn to keep some to yourself and in your heart.

These guys were looking for miracles and as they were waiting, Jesus came their way and they asked for their eyes to be healed. The miracles were imagined and created in their hearts and as they were looking for it, their miracles were also looking for them. It was also their mindset that led Christ to their vicinity, and they cried out for their miracle, and He gave it to them.

It does not matter where you are, your miracles will always find you. Miracles work by faith. If you do not believe it, you may not get it because it works with expectations. The Lord could not do many miracles in Galilee, His hometown because of their unbelief.

Some people with special grace do get miracles without knowing what happened to them because intercessors are always praying for the sick, poor, oppressed, barren, orphans, widows, widowers, churches, governments, and name it. Even with that, most of those who received the miracles are mainly those who believe in the intervention of the power of God in their lives and at the same time think good or positively.

Luke 11:20 says, "But if I with the finger of God cast out devils, no doubt the kingdom of God has come upon you." Create and develop the mindset where you can be seeing, imaging, or imagining yourself casting out the devils. Start seeing in your spiritual eyes or imagination that the Kingdom of God has come upon you.

Begin to see the Kingdom of God where you have a peaceful life, one where you will live forever in God's Kingdom where you will not taste lack or scarcity, sickness, and death. "A land which the LORD thy God careth for the eyes of the LORD thy God are always upon it, from the beginning of the year even unto the end of the year." Deuteronomy 11:12 (KJV).

The Lord our God takes delight in the prosperity of His servants. I believe that this is our portion as children of God because we are joint heirs with Christ and His righteousness is of us for, He has conquered witchcraft, poverty, diseases, and death for us forever.

"O death, where is thy sting? O grave, where is thy victory? The sting of death is sin, and the strength of sin is the law. But thanks be to God, which giveth us the victory through our Lord Jesus Christ." 1 Corinthians 15:55-57 (KJV).

You don't have victory until you believe that you have received it. It is only a function of the mind, a belief system. You cannot get what you do not believe that you have already received.

It is no illusion; you must believe in them and create them in your heart for them to manifest in your life. Thoughts vibrate to actualize an objective or strategy. I pray that the Lord will open the eyes of your understanding to see.

"And Elisha prayed, and said, LORD, I pray thee, open his eyes, that he may see. And the LORD opened the eyes of the young man; and he saw: and behold, the mountain was full of horses and chariots of fire round about Elisha." 2 Kings 6:17 (KJV).

Look at how Elisha was confident of his victory because he was a spiritual man. He walked in the spirit and saw his revelations. His servant could not see in the spirit and cried to his master as the enemies surrounded them. Therefore, fear not for those with us are more than those who are against us. Praise God!

The man of God prayed to God to open his eyes so that he could see the horses and chariots of fire round about him. There are horses and chariots of fire round about you more than your enemies. In other words, those armies or soldiers who are fighting your courses are much more than the few fighting against you. Those fighting your courses are more than your enemies by more than a millionfold.

You are therefore always a winner, an overcomer and more than a conqueror. Let me tell you a simple fact. There are a few lawbreakers on Earth. It is the same people that circulate in the prisons.

However, some people have negative imaginations to commit mostly financial crimes which they may or may not be able to perform or do negative witchcraft which cannot work. Those that go to prison are just notorious for themselves and they are few compared to the population of good people.

They go in and come out and in no time, they go back again. There are many more law-abiding citizens on earth than criminals, which may account for less than three per cent. "For whom hath known the mind of the Lord that he may instruct him? But we have the mind of Christ." I Corinthians 2:16 (KJV).

Remember that we are made in God's image and likeness as spirits living in the flesh. If you walk in the spirit, of your Father, then He will reveal to you great and mighty things which you did not know (Please see Jeremiah 33:3).

A good Christian should be able to think, visualize, picture, mirror, or imagine or create in his mind good and great things. Your life's journey must be planned and executed in your mind. It is the images that you have created in your mind's eyes that you will be seeing as your dreams and visions and confessing them into being in the physical realm, in the same manner, the Father created the heaven and the earth. Those thoughts and imaginations are the visions that will propel your life.

You need to know the Word of God because the Father is in His Word. Meditate on them and speak to yourself until you become part of the Word of God or like it and the Father will be revealing Himself to you and you become like His Christ and have that mindset of Christ.

"But unto them which are called, both Jews and Greeks, Christ the power of God, and the wisdom of God. Because the foolishness of God is wiser than men, and the weakness of God is stronger than men." 1 Corinthians 1:24-25 (KJV).

Of course, when you have that mindset of Christ, you cannot see any more limits. When you see five loaves of bread and two fish, you will immediately know it will be more than enough for five thousand men plus their women and children and some baskets full of leftovers. Praise God!

Anything outside the plan and will of God for you must be cast down, particularly when you see them in your dreams or visions or your mind's eyes because at this level you should be walking in the spirit and not in the flesh. Be more careful of what comes out of your mouth because eating with an unwashed hand will not defile the man. What goes into it is not capable of defiling the man but what comes out of it.

Matthew 12:36-37 says, "But I say unto you, that every idle word that men shall speak, they shall give account thereof in the day of judgment. By thy words, thou shalt be justified, and by thy words, thou shalt be condemned." Your enemies will be standing by, and you may not see them. But any idle words that you speak, they will carry it and use it against you.

Remember when the devil was passing with the angels and the Lord asked him where he was coming from, and he told the Lord that he was coming from the earth where he went to deceive His people? The Lord asked him if he saw His Servant Job, a righteous and upright man and he said that Job was as such because He gave him everything.

What I am driving at is that if you do not do, say, or utter any evil from your mouth, they will not have anything against you because they work only with what you have done or said. A man is very often justified or condemned by the word of his mouth because out of the abundance of the heart the mouth speaks.

However, the Lord may allow them to try you, but you must surely overcome them because you are an overcomer, and the Lord will also at that time raise a standard for you and make an escape route for you. When they come like the flood against you the Lord shall raise a standard against them. therefore, they cannot succeed. Praise God!

"And the LORD said unto Satan, whence comes thou? Then Satan answered the LORD, and said, from going to and from in the earth, and from walking up and down in it. And the LORD said unto Satan, Hast thou considered my servant Job, that there is none like him in the earth, a perfect and an upright man, one that feared God, and eschewed evil? Then Satan answered the LORD, and said, Doth Job fear God for nought?" Job 1:7-9 (KJV).

No one fears God for nothing but for our benefit, He is our Father and the source of wisdom and life.

You must always allow the Lord to direct your steps with His instructions and not rely on your understanding.

Listen to your emotions and know when the Lord is talking to you. Glue yourself to the Word of God. Allow Him to rule you so that you can have the best of life. Do not look at your current situation or your reality.

Begin to see yourself as a new creature in Christ and the former things have passed away and all things have become new. Start imagining your new life and then there shall come forth new songs and languages.

"I waited patiently for the LORD, and he inclined unto me, and heard my cry. He brought me up also out of a horrible pit, out of the miry clay, and set my feet upon a rock, and established my goings. And he hath put a new song in my mouth, even praise unto our God: many shall see it, and fear, and shall trust in the LORD." Psalm 40:1-3 (KJV).

No matter what the enemies have done or doing, the Lord shall deliver us from them and establish our goings. The people shall see what the Lord has done and rejoice and sing praises on your behalf. Praise God!

And you will be speaking and singing to yourself a new song, 'I am the bread of life.' 'I am the living water, whosoever that drink of me shall thirst no more.' 'I am the light of the world whosoever that follows me shall not walk in darkness,' and more of it. See now that you have gotten your eyes therefore you are full of light.

You become a revelation to yourself and the world because the Lord is with you and working with you and in you. For the Lord is now a lamp to your feet and a torch unto your paths. There is always light wherever you go and even in darkness arises light.

"The lamp of the body is the eye. If therefore your eye is good, your whole body will be full of light." Matthew 6:22 (KJV). You must see from your mind and focus as to where you are coming from and where you are going. If you do not know where you are going, you will not know when you will get there and even when you get there or where you started.

You cannot derail or go wrong. Somebody who has no spiritual mind cannot understand what you are talking about, hear what you are hearing, or see what you are seeing.

When you start walking at this level and have the mind of Christ, you will have greater revelations, unmerited favours shall follow you and you will begin to see new visions and new dreams because of the anointing, and every yoke shall be destroyed, and you'll move from ordinary to extraordinary.

They are the mysteries of the Kingdom which has been revealed unto us. But they will see and not perceive and hear and will not understand because they are not spiritually decerned like us.

"But as it is written, 'Eye hath not seen, nor ear heard, neither have entered into the heart of man, the things which God hath prepared for them that love him.' But God hath revealed them unto us by his Spirit. "For the Spirit searches all things, yea, the deep things of God." I Corinthians 2:9-10 (KJV).

When you know the Word, imagine it, and speak it. The Lord will begin to reveal Himself to you, those things which the eyes have not seen before, nor the ears heard.

Those things which have never at any time entered the heart of man, the Lord will be putting them into your heart and they, in turn, become your dreams and visions and imaginations because you will be seeing them with the eyes of your spirit, and they will begin to look normal to you. For they are part of the secrets of the Kingdom.

Take an example from Christ when He used five loaves of bread and two fishes to feed the five thousand. He believed and imagined the multiplier effect in God's word and prayed and it came to pass. He was not just seeing five loaves of bread and two fish, but thousands of loaves and fish, enough to feed the five thousand men and their families and some baskets leftover in His spiritual eyes. Otherwise, He wouldn't have tried it. It is a function of faith or belief system.

As they have not existed before, you begin to imagine them and command them into being and they shall come to be. Greatness, success, victory, and failure are all concepts in the heart of man and will depend on how you manipulate or manage them. Look, you are the son of God, the King of all kings.

"I call heaven and earth to record this day against you, that I have set before you life and death, blessing and cursing: therefore, choose life, that both thou and thy seed may live": Deuteronomy 30:19 (KJV). You have everything laid down for you on the table to choose from.

Lifestyle is a choice because your destiny is in your hands. The Lord has asked you to choose for yourself what you want, life, death, curses, or blessing. You can do well to choose a good life or blessing for yourself and your family.

It is all a belief system, or mindset to create your life in your mind and NOT what other people are thinking, and talking about you but what you say about yourself will stand. Declare aloud:

- I am of royal blood, the son of God.
- I am born of God and not of the flesh and blood.
- I am here to reign!
- I define my destiny; I am highly blessed and favoured!
- Praise God!

"Let us hold fast the confession of our hope without wavering, for He who promised is faithful." Hebrews 10:23 (NKJV). Declare the area in which you will be reigning either in education, commerce, engineering, ministry, business, banking, etc. And keep speaking it and do not stop. Keep up with your confession even in any situation in life. PRAISE GOD!

4: A Man Reaps What He Sows

There is time and season for everything under the sun and man cannot change or alter it. There is time to work and time to get paid, time to plant and time to harvest, time to merry and time to mourn, a time to sleep and a time to wake, and so on.

Everything or seed is sown according to time or season and the same applies to the harvest. A child has a set time to go to school to acquire knowledge and skills to prepare him for the future and a set time or season to apply the acquired knowledge, skills and understanding.

"To everything, there is a season, and a time to every purpose under the heaven: A time to be born, and a time to die; a time to plant, and a time to pluck up that which is planted; A time to kill, and a time to heal; a time to break down, and a time to build up.

A time to weep, and a time to laugh; a time to mourn, and a time to dance; A time to cast away stones, and a time to gather stones together; a time to embrace, and a time to refrain from embracing.

A time to get, and a time to lose; a time to keep, and a time to cast away; A time to rend, and a time to sew; a time to keep silence, and a time to speak; A time to love, and a time to hate; a time of war, and a time of peace." Ecclesiastes 3:1-8 (KJV).

There is a time for everything including a time to gather and time to scatter. You can embrace anything like ministry, business, marriage, relationship, or anything you may wish to but there might be times when you must let go.

You can recall that the Bible says that if one eye will lead you to hell, you plug it off. You are better off entering into heaven with one eye than going to hell with two eyes. Again, we can also recall that you cannot be unequally yoked together because righteousness has nothing to do with evil, or darkness and light.

"Be ye not unequally yoked together with unbelievers: for what fellowship hath righteousness with unrighteousness? and what communion hath light with darkness?" 2 Corinthians 6:14 (KJV).

In times of war, you turn your ploughshares into swords. At peacetime you convert your sword to ploughshares and spears into pruning hooks. It is the season and time that determines the situation in the environment.

You must understand that your battle is not against flesh and blood but against powers, principalities, and spiritual wickedness in high places. The battle is in your heart from conception, planning, and the final victory. Beat your ploughshares into swords and your pruninghooks into spears: let the weak say, I am strong. Joel 3:10 (KJV).

Whatsoever you sow will come from your mind and anything you sew in your mind becomes your imagination, dreams or visions thus creating your life, reality, or victory. Those things you think, imagine, meditate, and visualise become your life as thoughts create reality. That is the common saying of the Bible which says as a man thinketh in his heart so is he.

When you think good about a person or people, that good or love will depart from your heart to the people you are blessing with love and manifest in them without you saying a word or even before you say it.

In the same manner, that love will come back to you and glow or spark in love and peace in you. You can now see how a man can reap whatsoever he sows. When that person sees you, you will see the expression of love from him because his spirit has received your love and is returning the same to you, the law of reciprocity.

In the same way, if you sow hatred in your heart against a person or group, that hatred becomes witchcraft and goes after the person or people even before you start your incantations and spells.

This is very wicked particularly when it comes from someone very close to you causing you to absorb evil spirits and negative energy. In the same manner, the evil or wicked spirit will come back to you. When you show mercy, it will come back to you even your family.

It should not be encouraged. Sometimes when they are not getting a quick result, they go directly to the witch or black magic doctors to help them with their evil enterprise.

Prayer:

- I uproot, destroy, and return to sender(s) any evil imagination, thoughts, and incantation against me and my family back to senders.
- As many as gathered, as many as consented, as many as connived, as many as cast spells, as many as spoke evils, as many as meditated, as many as imagined, as many as agreed, let their evil imagination fall upon them, let their evil meditation fall upon them, let their evil pronouncements fall upon them, let their wickedness fall upon them.
- Any evil devised shall go back to the senders in the mighty name of Jesus.
- Lord, do not allow the evil people to prosper in their evils.
- No divination, premonition, and enchantment against us shall prosper in Jesus' name, amen.

Your mind or heart is the command or control centre of your life. We must therefore, guide, filter, and screen whatsoever that goes into it because whatever we think and say becomes part of us and our lives. "Keep thy heart with all diligence; for out of it are the issues of life." Proverbs 4:23 (KJV).

Now you can see your heart as your garden or farm where all your seeds are planted and ready for harvest. You can also see it as your storehouse or warehouse where all your stuff is stored. In which you can harvest, reap, or take from your stock.

Everything comes from the heart because it is the command-and-control tower of our aeroplanes. You cannot do anything without it coming from your heart. However, you may not have had a good thought of it before implementing it, but it is still from your heart without appropriate planning or thought. Where there is no vision, the people perish.

Your dreams and visions must be planned, measurable, and executable from your heart. In other words, you must set goals for your dreams and visions. Every good, successful, and delightful person thinks good, success, and peace in his heart but an evil person thinks evil and that is what he is. Whatsoever a man conceives in his heart is what he becomes and manifests in his attitude, behaviour, and life.

"A good man out of the good treasure of his heart bringeth forth that which is good; and an evil man out of the evil treasure of his heart bringeth forth that which is evil: for of the abundance of the heart his mouth speaks." Luke 6:45 (KJV).

"Finally, brethren, whatsoever things are true, whatsoever things are honest, whatsoever things are just, whatsoever things are pure, whatsoever things are lovely, whatsoever things are of good report; if there be any virtue, and if there be any praise, think on these things. Those things, which ye have both learned, and received, and heard, and seen in me, do and the God of peace shall be with you." Philippians 4:8-9 (KJV).

In conclusion, anything you say or do will surely come back to you and even if they are any praises, they will still come back to you. Therefore, whatsoever a man sows he shall reap.

Now pray:

Oh Lord, let the meditation of my heart and words of my mouth be acceptable in thy sight, oh Lord my God, my strength and redeemer! Psalm 19:14

5: Victory

Victory is a word of conquest, triumph, winning, to conquer, to overcome or succeed. It is a language of war or warriors. This is a term, that is applied to combat. or warfare and often used when we overcome or triumph over the enemies. Following a war or combat the successful or winning side is the victorious side and that is our victory.

A victory is an act of winning or defeating your enemies on the battlefield, winning a competition or game. It is being successful or a success in an endeavour or an event. The triumphant soldiers are the victorious ones because it is a military term.

We are always on the war front, not fighting against flesh and blood but against powers, principalities and spiritual wickedness in high places. In this war, we do not have many options but to win because our God is our victory. He is the winner for us or our Winner.

You are an incorruptible being like your Father and cannot lose a war or fight. An example is Jesus who went through the grave and conquered death and the grave could not hold him captive. He conquered death for all believers and gave us victory for all times because death is the last enemy of man which has now been conquered or crushed as the stink of death is sin which has also been crushed as the stink of sin is law which has been conquered by grace.

"Finally, my brethren, be strong in the Lord, and in the power of his might. Put on the whole armour of God, that ye may be able to stand against the wiles of the devil.

For we wrestle not against flesh and blood, but against principalities, against powers, against the rulers of the darkness of this world, against spiritual wickedness in high places. Wherefore take unto you the whole armour of God, that ye may be able to withstand in the evil day, and having done all, to stand." Ephesians 6:10-13 (KJV).

However, the Lord conquered the last enemy, which is death for man, but we should not relax and think that it is all over. It is not just because the devil himself is still roaring all over the earth seeking for those to devour to join him in his hell. He doesn't want to be alone and that is why he has been applying the same strategy as in the Garden of Eden where he used Mama Eve to get Papa Adam.

You must learn to apply wisdom in whatever you are doing because he can also use your spouse to bring you down in whatever you are doing including your career and family. He can also use your boss, friends, relatives, or neighbours. You must not rely on your wisdom but allow the Lord to guide you and direct your steps.

You must be strong in the might of the Lord which is His word by knowing and applying it with wisdom. He can use anybody to get you to think evil or negatively and fall for the small temptation. The armour is the word of salvation to save and protect you because it is the truth that you know that will set or make you free.

They are spiritual wickedness in high places and would come in diverse scams to lure you, please protect everything about you with the armour of God so that you will be able to withstand their evil day.

You must have your loins or everything about you girt or covered with the truth of righteousness because you have been made righteous by faith through the shedding of the blood of the

Lamb and His subsequent resurrection from death, which is a victory for all believers, provided you belief in your heart and confess with your mouth that He is the Lord of your life.

All wars are never canal but spiritual and are fought, won, or lost in the heart which is in the spirit. You must take the shield of faith to be able to conquer or win them. They will adopt some tactics and strategies to corrupt you through fear but do not give in to their devices because greater is He that is in you than them.

You already have the helmet of salvation which is the Christ in you and your faith to quench the arrows and fiery darts of the enemies. Finally, you must use that sword of the Spirit which is the Word of God to destroy all their evils and other strategies and you gain victory. If you know the power and authority in you, you will know that you are living in victory because all things are yours as Christ is the Lord's.

People do not know you because they do not know your Father, if they knew you, they would have also known your Father because you are the son and image of your Father, and you are in your Father and your Father is in you. Praise God!!

"I have set the LORD always before me: because he is at my right hand, I shall not be moved. Therefore, my heart is glad, and my glory rejoices: my flesh also shall rest in hope. For thou wilt not leave my soul in hell; neither wilt thou suffer thine Holy One to see corruption." Psalm 16:8-10 (KJV). You are one with your Father, therefore you cannot be perturbed.

You are His temple, and He dwells in you and you in Him therefore you cannot be afraid of what man can do unto you. Spiritual battles are fought, won, or lost in the heart. Now your heart is glad, and your glory rejoices because He will not allow you to see any defeat or loss in the war. Your heart is glad for He has given you victory, and you are the winner.

Declare: I am the winner! Praise God!!

You cannot see corruption because you are incorruptible as His holy one. He will always lead you in His part of righteousness and you live in peace and happiness because you are always in His presence. Your righteousness and incorruptibility are not of your righteousness or merit but of grace because of the righteousness of God through Christ.

Your grace or unmerited favour is of faith in the belief that you have received them. It is your divine gift from the Father and no one can take it away from you because no one is justified by work but by grace.

"Knowing that a man is not justified by the works of the law, but by the faith of Jesus Christ, even we have believed in Jesus Christ, that we might be justified by the faith of Christ, and not by the works of the law: for by the works of the law shall no flesh be justified." Galatians 2:16 (KJV).

You are the grace of God and His righteousness. The faith and righteousness of Christ are more than sufficient for you because you may not have enough faith but as little as a mustard seed will do. You were made strong through His weakness, made rich through His poverty and by His stripes you were healed.

You need only believe in the Lord and tell Him the victory you are looking for and He is always delightful in the prosperity and victory of His people. You only need to trust Him, and the battle will be His and victory is yours. His name is 'I AM', meaning He is what you want him to be at that material time. 'I AM' means I AM your healer when you need healing, I AM your righteousness when you a wet or soaked in sin because where sin abounds His grace abounds more. I AM your victory in times of defeat and war.

"And God said unto Moses, I Am That I Am: and he said, thus shalt thou say unto the children of Israel, I Am hath sent me unto you. And God said moreover unto Moses, thus shalt thou say unto the children of Israel, the Lord God of your fathers, the God of Abraham, the God of Isaac, and the God of Jacob, hath sent me unto you: this is my name forever, and this is my memorial unto all generations." Exodus 3:14-15 (KJV).

He appeared to Moses as a deliverer, when they became hungry and thirsty, He became their provider and so on and that is who He is to all generations.

Incorruptibility, defeat, or decay cannot be near you because it is your will which is the will of God for you. When you ask you must receive an answer, you seek you find and for everyone that knocked it shall be opened unto him. And that is your victory for you have overcome the world. Praise God.

When you seek and there are carpets and chairs, you must move them and look well. Even if there are rubbles, you must move them depending on what you are looking for.

That is an example of how to seek and in the same manner you will ask and bang if the knock is not loud enough which may involve some selective fasting and prayers. I have searched the dictionary of God and there is no such word as 'defeat' except to conquer or defeat the enemies. There is nothing like 'no' but 'yes.' I can do all things through Christ who strengthens me. With Him all things are possible.

Every 'victory' is possible both in the physical and spiritual because they are all fought and won in the spiritual before they start to manifest in the physical. He never lost any wars and if He is for us nobody can be against us. You may feel the vibration here, but the actual battle is carried out in the spiritual realm by His heavenly hosts according to the strength of your faith.

After the creation of the earth, the first victory was experienced by God when He overcame darkness with light. He was able to overcome darkness with light because He saw light in His dreams, visions, spiritual eyes, and imaginations and created it in His mind.

After creating the earth, He could not see the light and He paused His creative activities and commanded the light to come forth before He continued. You cannot get what you cannot see or know about.

When Abraham and Lot parted, the Lord asked Abraham to look up and he did. The Lord said to him, as much land as you can see, that I have given to you and your offspring for your possession forever, and He asked him to step on them and possess them. The more he went stepping his foot on them, the more land he saw and claimed. You must see something before you can start thinking of possessing them. Genesis 13:14.

Victory is a function of the mind. It is faith or a belief system. You must believe in it and that you are able or even more than able. Joshua and Caleb were able to enter the Promised Land because they did not see themselves as grasshoppers in the face of the giants but as giants before the grasshoppers. But as those whose God can do exceedingly abundantly more than they can reasonably think or expect. The exceedingly and abundantly are the power of faith that works in you.

All twelve tribal leaders and spies who assessed or scoped out the promised land for 40 days saw the same thing. Joshua and Caleb saw the same thing as the other ten. The difference is that Joshua and Caleb looked at God's promises and saw that there were armies and difficulties, but God could bring them deliverance and victory. Amid difficulty or oppression there must be something great or great opportunity for the favoured and faithful. Amid famine, someone will plant, and it would yield seventy, hundred folds and dig a well and have water. You may ask how, but Isaac had it (Genesis 26:1-5).

Whereas the other 10, all they could see were the problems, challenges, and difficulties. It all depends on how they looked at it. Joshua and Caleb saw it given the promises of God with the mindset that with God all things are possible or one with God is with the majority.

They saw the giants in the land as bread for them and concluded that their defence had already departed from them and that the Lord had given them the land and that they will possess it, not by their arrow or spear but that the Lord of Heaven has given it to them according to His promise.

"Only rebel not ye against the Lord, neither fear ye the people of the land; for they are bread for us: their defence is departed from them, and the Lord is with us: fear them not." Numbers 14:9.

Victory is a mental attitude with the absence of fear of loss or defeat. Victory is a spirit that you must create and develop in your heart. It is the spirit to overcome, the ideology of boldness, and the spirit of can do, that have done attitude of victory and triumph.

Joshua and Caleb among the spies saw that the land was good and flowing with milk and honey. You cannot be afraid of your enemies because you do not know how afraid or fearful they are of you.

When you see a small boy standing up to a giant, know that he has something behind him, and the greatest is faith because man can always fail you but the Lord will never fail you.

As the Lord is with you, He will put more fears into them. Victory is always a function of the mind that is why you have a lot of war propaganda when nations are arising against each other. When they get you to falter, they have won and that is not your portion because they are the ones to falter as the Lord hands the victory to you. Praise God!!

In addition, they saw themselves possessing the land without shooting an arrow or by their strength. Joshua and Caleb saw victory, conquest, triumph, winning, and success in their visions, dreams, and imaginations, in the eyes of their minds and meditated on them, believed in them, and spoke and the Lord heard them and agreed with them, and they possessed the promised land.

There is no way you can get what you do not believe in. All battles and wars are never physical but spiritual even kingdoms against kingdoms, neighbours against and even in the families.

Of course, you believe, if your grace and righteousness are not sufficient for you that of the King Christ will be more than enough for you. I have done much counselling and prayed for many things and people, in most if not all the cases I handed it over to the Lord and let His will be done and I found out that the will of the Lord is our will to achieve our desired result which could be marriage, immigration papers, healing or some form of breakthroughs. Praise God!!

Those who said that they were going to die in the wilderness without reaching the promised land all died because they were not able to get the victory, their carcasses were left in the wilderness because the Lord said, 'As you say, so I will do to you.' Numbers 14:28.

There is no way your enemies can overcome you unless you agree with them and give them that option. Joshua and Caleb exhibited the spirit of power, boldness, and of sound mind without any atom of fear and stood on the promises of God. That is all we need to be victorious and to cultivate the spirit of victory, dwell in victory, carry victory and think victory, meditate on victory, and walk on victory.

The ministry of Jesus is focused on repentance. Repentance is the activity of reviewing one's actions and feeling contrition or regret for past wrongs. It generally involves a commitment to personal change and resolving to live a more responsible and humane life by thinking and behaving like Him. He is proactive in whatever He decides to do and even imagine doing. He did not contemplate failure or defeat because it was not an option for Him.

He never feared anybody but walked out of trouble when it came. At the point of death, they asked Him if He was the King of the Jews. He answers them 'You said I am. For this reason, I was born.'

John 18:37 says, "Pilate, therefore, said unto him, Art thou a king then? Jesus answered Thou sayest that I am a king. To this end was I born, and for this cause came I into the world, that I should bear witness unto the truth. Every one that is of the truth heareth my voice."

Jesus is always committed to speaking the truth and it is that truth that made Him free and gave Him victory over sin and death. You are the king and nothing has the power or authority to hold you captive or enslave you except fear and doubts. This is your kingdom, and you are born to reign in the Father's kingdom for all things are yours. Your victory is in the truth and the truth is what gives you the freedom and triumph.

It does not matter what your enemies are thinking or saying. All they are looking for is how to bring you down and win over you. Of course, they have failed, because they can only win or overcome you if you allow them through fear, doubts, and ignorance. No one has the right to take anything that belongs to you except if you give it to them freely or out of fear.

They cannot take whatever is yours because they will be afraid of the consequences both here on earth and in the world to come. Victory is often taken and not given. The Bible says, 'Since the time of John the Baptist, the heavens suffer violence, and violence taketh it by force.'

They can only win and take victory when you surrender out of fear or ignorance. Remember that those with you are more than those against you and anyone with God is with the majority. Therefore, you are the winner, and the victory is yours. I will give you a few examples of when He was informed of the sickness of His friend Lazarus, He did not accept death for His friend and declared that 'the sickness is not unto death.'

When He eventually died, He said, 'He was sleeping.' When He went there the sisters saw Him and said, 'If You had been there, our brother would not have died.' He said to them, 'If you believe, you will see the glory of God.' Jesus was always seeing a healthy living Lazarus and not a dead man.

He never conceived or imagined death for Lazarus His friend. When His disciples persisted, He told them that he was dead even though He did not want to conceive it in His heart. Then there comes a question of fact and truth.

"These things said he: and after that, he saith unto them, "Our friend Lazarus sleepiest; but I go, that I may awake him out of sleep. Then said his disciples, Lord, if he sleeps, he shall do well. Howbeit Jesus spoke of his death: but they thought that he had spoken of taking of rest in sleep. Then said Jesus unto them plainly, Lazarus is dead." John 11:11-14 KJV.

When He saw the people crying, He was touched, and 'He wept.' Asked to be shown where they laid him and He said, "Father, I thank thee that thou hast heard me. And I know that thou hearest me always: but because of the people which stand by I said it, that they may believe that thou hast sent me."

And He called Lazarus forth, and he came forth and He asked them to lose him and let him go. Brother Lazarus was rapped with grave clothes, and He asked them to lose him to go.

Many people are trapped in fear which cannot allow them to get victory. Some of you are suffering from blindness and cannot see or see and cannot perceive. They hear and cannot understand. I pray that the veil or anything that is covering your eyes so that you cannot see and perceive or hear and understand or hold you captive, be loosed and let you go in the mighty name of Jesus, amen.

"That seeing they may see, and not perceive, and hearing they may hear, and not understand; lest at any time they should be converted, and their sins should be forgiven them." Mark 4:12 (KJV). Foolishness is in their mindset and that is why they can see and cannot perceive or hear and cannot understand. This group of people needs a deliverance, rethink, repentance, or a change of mental attitude or heart.

He said that Lazarus was not dead but was sleeping when they asked Him what happened to him. He knew that a sleeping person can always wake up from sleep, but the dead person cannot get up.

He never imagined or pronounced Lazarus dead because as a man thinketh in his heart so is he, and when you decree a thing, it shall be established. The Lord said to the children of Israel what you say I will do to you.

If He had agreed that Lazarus was dead, then it would have been difficult to bring him back to life. This is part of the secrets or mysteries of the Kingdom being revealed to us.

Now let us take some prayers:

- In the mighty name of Jesus, a name above all other names, I bind any spirit that may want to hinder or kill my prayers from getting an immediate answer.
- I bind them and they remain bound while I receive and manifest all my benefits and miracles.
- I command any demons that are causing me to see and not perceive to die by fire.
- I command demons that are causing me to hear and not understand to die by fire.
- I command any witchcraft spirit that is trying to derail my destiny to die by fire.
- I command any evil spirit that is delaying my progress to die by fire including its sources and foundation.
- I command any evil spirit against my family to die by fire now.
- I command any negative spirit against my ministry, business, and job to die by fire now.
- I decree and declare that every demonic agenda to bury my destiny on the ground must die by fire in the Mighty name of Jesus.
- Every evil gathering where my name or my family is mentioned must receive the thunder and fire of the Holy Ghost now.
- Thank you, Lord, for fighting our battles in the mighty name of Jesus, amen.

Brother Lazarus was tied or wrapped with grave clothes and that spirit of grave clothes was removed or lost out of him for him to get on with his life again. Now we are going to pray so that any grave clothes or anything they have used to tie you, your destiny down or hold you captive must lose you now:

- I decree and declare that any grave clothes that they have tied us and held us captive like Lazarus must lose your host now and let us go.
- Any spirit of infirmity or disease that has tied you down must lose you now and let you go in the mighty name of Jesus.
- Any spirit of poverty that has tied you down, stopping your destiny must lose your host and let you go now.
- Any spirit of confusion that has tied you down that is delaying your God's calling must die now and lose you and let you go now.
- Any spirit of delay fighting your progress or destiny in life must die now and lose you to go in the mighty name of Jesus.
- Any spirit of envy that is causing people to hate you even stopping your destiny helpers must die now by fire and let you go.
- Any contrary spirit that is planted in your life must lose your host now to go and fulfil God's calling in you now.
- Any spirit of barrenness that has tired you down must lose you to go now.
- Any spirit of singleness that has tired you down must lose you now to go.
- Any spirit of unemployment that has tired you down must lose you now to go.
- Any spirit of strangulation in your life must lose you now.
- Any spirit of failure attached to you that is causing havoc in your life must lose you to go now.

- Any spirit of lack of favour that has tired you down must lose you to go now and receive your favour.
- Lose your host now and let him go.
- Lose your host now and let him go.
- Lose your host now and let him go.
- Lose your host now and let him go.
- Lose your host now and let him go.
- Lose your host now and let him go.
- You're free to go.
- Go, go, go, go, go, go, go, go, go, go, go, go!
- I decree and confess that divine favour must find me now.
- I decree and declare that the will of the Father must be fulfilled in my life, and I possess my possession now in Jesus' mighty name I pray. amen.

Jesus is always having a positive attitude to life and is always bold and with a sound mind. He is the greatest visionary, greatest success, the Word of God which became Flesh and dwelt among men.

When He was talking about His death and resurrection, He was focusing on His resurrection and not on death. He was seeing Himself coming out of the grave victoriously. That was His vision and dream, and He did not stop meditating and declaring them.

That is the victory which He had over death and has conquered it forever for us all. The Bible says, 'That Spirit which brought Christ up from the grave is in us.' If He is in you? What are you doing with it? Are you exhibiting it in your life as a Christian? A Spirit which can quicken anything even the dead.

"But if the Spirit of him that raised Jesus from the dead dwells in you, he that raised Christ from the dead shall also quicken your mortal bodies by his Spirit that dwelleth in you." Romans 8:11 (KJV).

That Spirit which raised Christ from death is an extraordinary conquering, victorious Spirit which conquered man's greatest enemy which is death and the shame of it and the agony and reproach it brings.

The Spirit of resurrection, triumph and victory are in us. This Spirit is in us. Did you at any time see yourself as triumphant, successful, or victorious? You can only be more than a conqueror when you begin to see yourself as such in your spirit and start having mental images of yourself as more than a conqueror, a victor, and a success.

Jesus is a positive thinker and speaker, with a positive imagination who never believed that anything is impossible and at the same time, He walks in righteousness and speaks righteousness.

Righteousness did not just end in not stealing, avoiding fornication and the rest of them. The greatest sin is lying to yourself, and the greatest lies are being negative and fearful.

A negative mental attitude is the worst sin and the worst unrighteousness. It is deceit and scam and is not from God. Righteousness is having an excellent spirit that goes with the right and positive mental attitude. You cannot be righteous and be a person with a negative mental attitude or bad mindset.

The right mental attitude is 'faith' and the Bible says, 'it is impossible to please God without faith.' When He was in a boat with His disciples there was this big storm while He was sleeping and His disciples woke Him up and said, 'Master we are perishing.' He commanded the storm 'Peace, be still,' and there was a great calm (Mark 4:39). The disciples wondered what manner of man He was that even the winds obeyed Him. The power and authority are in the mind when you believe in your heart, and you confess with your mouth. Jesus is the Word of God; He believed in them and confessed them.

He did not waver or doubt His ability or the ability of His Father to do exceedingly and abundantly above those we can think of or imagine. You are in the Father and the Father is in you to do exploits. The Lord even confessed that greater works shall you do if you believe. It is the same Jesus and the same Spirit of Truth that is operating to date. You can do it even greater because the victory is already yours. You are the winner and more than a conqueror! Praise God!!

I spoke to a man of God and He said to me, 'That is Jesus. You are not Jesus.' He forgot the most important part of the gospel where Jesus says, 'Those that believe in Me and the works that I did, greater works shall they do.

"Verily, verily, I say unto you, He that believeth on me, the works that I do shall he do also; and greater works than these shall he do, because I go unto my Father. And whatsoever ye shall ask in my name, that will I do, that the Father may be glorified in the Son. If ye shall ask anything in my name, I will do it." John 14:12-14 (KJV).

The victory of Jesus is in you and even greater victory shall you have if you can only believe. Jesus came to earth as the Son of God and any son of God can do the same. Those that believe, to them He hath given the power to become sons of God.

You can do like Jesus, even greater works depending on the power that worketh in you. When He was in the wilderness and hungry, the devil approached and asked Him to turn stone into bread. He replied, 'Man shall not live by bread alone, but by every word that proceeded from the mouth of God.'

The issue here is that many of us will give in to having the bread because we are hungry, without minding how the bread came about. That type of bread will often give temporary relief from hunger and immediately after, the worst will strike. We need to think ahead and plan like our Lord Jesus and that is the more reason why we should endeavour to have His type of mind and walk, talk, and think like Him.

Microwave fixes do not work for long but the blessing of the Lord maketh rich and adds no sorrow. You do not give in to eating microwaved bread because you are very hungry and looking for a quick fix or solution.

Wait for the living bread because the Father has seen your situation. He is there for you and shall make a way for you even where there seems to be no way. The living bread is one which you will eat and feel hungry no more. That is as you are finishing one bread, another is already there from the same source. Praise God!

He is 'Abba father', the Greatest provider, the maker of heaven and the earth. 'And prove me now herewith, said the LORD of hosts if I will not open you the windows of heaven, and pour you out a blessing, that there shall not be room enough to receive it.' Malachi 3:10.

Jesus answered, and said unto her, "If thou knewest the gift of God, and who it is that saith to thee, give me to drink; thou wouldest have asked of him, and he would have given thee living water." John 4:10 (KJV).

The lady of Samaria did not know who was talking with her and she asked Him how He could get water from the well when He had no cup, and the well was deep. Jesus said to her, 'If only you knew the gift of God you will not ask Me for a cup and the person who is asking of you.'

If you knew the gift of God in your life and what He has deposited in you, you would not dream or imagine failure, defeat, or disappointment. There are successes, victory upon victory, grace to grace, favour to favour, and triumph, even superabundance in you even before the foundation of the world. You need to know them and walk in them. The Lord says, 'My people are destroyed for lack of knowledge. Hosea 4:6.

Listen carefully, if the Father could not spare His only begotten Son, but delivered Him up for us all, how shall He not with Him also freely give us all things? Roman 8:32. The Bible says, "The earth and the fullest are the Lord's and they that dwell on them." Psalm 24:1.

This earth and the fullest He had given up to adopt us to be joint heirs with Him in the Kingdom of the Father. In other words, this rich Prince gave them up for me and you and became poor so that we will become rich. He took our poverty, and we became the wealthy royals through Him. Even with that, He knew He could not become poor because of the enormity of the potentiality. Praise God!

The Son of God who knew no sin was made sin so that we became the righteousness of God. He took the strokes and lashes so that we will not fall sick again, therefore by His stripes, we were healed. He took the shame and humiliation at the cross at Calvary so that we will not suffer shame again but live and walk victoriously with our shoulders high.

He had no wife so you may have your wife or husband. He had no children so that we may have them more abundantly. He gave up everything so that we may have them and have them more abundantly. He gave us victory over sin, sickness, lack or poverty, bareness, and everything including death which is said to be man's greatest and last enemy.

They have no strings over us. "O death, where is thy sting? O grave, where is thy victory? The sting of death is sin, and the strength of sin is the law. But thanks be to God, which giveth us the victory through our Lord Jesus Christ." 1 Corinthians 15:55-57 (KJV).

The King of Glory has swallowed up death in victory. He has conquered death forever and given us victory over it and sin. The head of the gates was lifted, and the King of Glory went in and took the keys of hell and Hades in addition to the keys of heaven which He already had.

"Whom God hath raised, having loosed the pains of death: because it was not possible that he should be holden of it." Acts 2:24 (KJV). Here the sadness, shame, and pain of death have been taken away because death or the grave couldn't hold Him captive. He took the captivities of sin and death captive and conquered death, locked and took the keys of hell and hades with Him and ascended to heaven.

If it was impossible for death or the grave to hold the first Son of God captive, how can that death or grave hold the second or third sons of God captive? You, lawyers, may argue that sin and law of God and that Christ is not the minister of sin, but I put it to you that where law abounds, the grace of our Lord Jesus abounds much more (Romans 5:20).

That victory has been won once and for all times through our Lord Jesus Christ. There has been the death and resurrection of Brother Lazarus and some others. But that of our Lord Jesus is that of a righteous man who had everything and gave them up for us all and suffered the shame of crucifixion for us. He was made sin so that we might become the righteousness of God. Praise God!

This is a man who knew no sin. "For He made Him who knew no sin to be sin for us, that we might become the righteousness of God in Him." 2 Corinthians 5:21. The Bible tells us that 'He is in the Father and the Father is in Him and we are in Him and He is also in us.' John 14:11.

If Christ is in us and we are in Him as the Bible says, 'We are the temple of the Holy Spirit.' If we believe in this very powerful Word of God then we shall be able to overcome all obstacles, defeat all our enemies tread on serpents and scorpions and destroy all the powers of the enemies and nothing shall by any means hurt us.

We shall then walk from glory to glory like our Lord Jesus, even greater glory because He said greater works shall we do.

"And these signs shall follow them that believe; In my name shall they cast out devils; they shall speak with new tongues; They shall take up serpents; and if they drink any deadly thing, it shall not hurt them; they shall lay hands on the sick, and they shall recover." Mark 16:17-18 (KJV).

This is victory. It is a mindset or belief system. You cannot do or get what you do not believe in. It works by faith as faith in turn works through love.

It is not only because we have the power which is already in us because He is with us even until the end of time. "See, I have this day set thee over the nations and the kingdoms, to root out, and to pull down, and to destroy, and to throw down, to build, and to plant." Jeremiah 1:10 (KJV).

Your world is in your hands. The Father hath given you all things unto your care to bulldoze, uproot, pull down, tear down, and destroy anything which you do not want on earth and in your lives and to build, plant, and create those things which you want. Some of us will say it was said to Jeremiah or Jesus or may have been said to Rev. Tony Ekperechi. The Lord has set us over the nations to root out, pull down and destroy those strongholds in our minds or thought systems.

The fears and lies that the enemies have planted in our minds. Destroy those negative pictures and evil thoughts. Every negative reality of your current life is a falsehood from the pit of hell. They are not real or true even though you may be seeing them with your naked eyes. The enemies are only trying to use them to deceive you and lower your faith.

You can uproot any negative plants the enemies have planted in your life, destroy any evil temple your name or materials have been placed in, set ablaze any contrary spirit after your life or anything exalting itself above the knowledge of God, and take all your captivities captive.

The enemies' plans can only become true in your life when you decide to agree with their plans. These are the things that the scripture says you should bring them to submit themselves to the obedience of the Son of God. You do not believe or condone lies because they are sins from the pit of hell. Call anybody who says, 'you cannot do it or make it', a liar.

Of course, you can do it and make it. On the other hand, the scripture says, 'build and plant.' What is He asking you to build and plant and how can you do them?

Some of you who are into science know what metamorphosis means - a process of going from one stage to another in nature. Men do the same thing from baby to adulthood. It is a process of renewing your heart or thought system from the negative, unbelief nature to the more powerful positive nature.

To build or plant is a process of teaching your spirit man or your subconscious mind the things of God and creating a new belief system with a good mental or positive mental attitude. You do not think about the past that the enemies created in your world and begin to look at the things which are before you, thus forgetting the things which are behind.

"Brethren, I count not myself to have apprehended: but this one thing I do, forgetting those things which are behind, and reaching forth unto those things which are before." Philippians 3:13-14 (KJV).

You do not dwell on your reality or current condition. Think differently or do something differently, otherwise, you will be getting the same result or answer. Romans 12:2 says, "And be not conformed to this world: but be ye transformed by the renewing of your mind, that ye may prove what is that good, and acceptable, and perfect, will of God."

As you have done away with the spirit of lies, deceit, and fears, you need to build, plant, and cultivate the Spirit of love, prosperity, peace, truth, and that fruitage of the Holy Spirit. The Bible says, 'Above all, that you might be in good health and prosper as your soul prospered.'

He went on to say that every other thing may fail or cease but 'Love' will never cease or end because Love is God. When you renew your heart, the God of peace will abide in you, and you see the peace, goodness, and joy of the Lord.

Of course, I was like you when I was told something in the Spirit which was written in the Bible. I wouldn't agree with them because I consider them too good to be true. I would say they were referring to Jesus or Abraham and not me.

'Now it was not written for his sake alone, that it was imputed to him; But for us also, to whom it shall be imputed if we believe on him that raised Jesus our Lord from the dead.' Romans 4:23-24 (KJV).

Know from now that any blessings, favours, victories, successes, or anything good attributed to any man or son of God including Jesus is also imputed to you and me. Our Lord Jesus said, 'It is the Father's good pleasure to give you the Kingdom.' Luke 12:32.

We have the Kingdom when we receive it, imagine it, meditate on it, dwell on it, walk on it, and confess it. We have it and the victory which goes with it. Praise God! "For thou wilt not leave my soul in hell; neither wilt thou suffer Thine Holy One to see corruption." Psalms 16:10 (KJV). I was discussing this Psalm with a man of God and He told me that the Bible was referring to Jesus. Of course, that is correct.

Then who is Jesus? We all agree that He is the Son of God. The Firstborn of all creation. Now, who are you or I? We are also sons of God and all of us cannot be born at the same time and place. We were born according to the set time of God and cannot be of the same age and the same generation. Whatever is born of God is of God for what the Lord has prepared for His children must be given to us.

You are a son of God and a royal one, a king and priest born at such a time and place as this. A holy child redeemed and repurchased with His precious royal blood. Jesus was also a King and a priest born at such a time as that in Bethlehem, Judaea. His own time when He paved the way for us and showed us the way to victory.

It is the Father's good pleasure that we do not go near hell or see corruption. Every victory attributed to Abraham, Moses, Elijah, David, and our Lord Jesus is also imputed to us. We went through all those challenges including the death and resurrection of our Lord Jesus.

That was for us to know that we are more than conquerors and can overcome any situation because the greatest Spirit which quickens all things and raised Christ from death is in us. He took our sins and died for us, therefore, there will be no second death for us. Praise God!

Make a joyful noise and shout:

- I am the winner.
- I am more than a conqueror.
- I am a victorious one.
- I am here to reign!
- I can do all things through Christ who strengthens me!
- Praise God!!

Prayer:

- I declare and decree that I uproot, root out and bulldoze anything, any seed, or plant that the enemies have planted in my life in any occult altar in the land, sea, or any planet in the mighty name of Jesus.
- Anywhere they have taken our names, family name or destiny for evil, I destroy them now and call on the God of consuming fire to send the consuming fire to consume them, their evil altars, their sources, and foundations whether they are on the earth, under the earth, in the sea, under the sea and in whatever planet they may be located or hiding.
- I break, uproot, destroy bulldoze and set the children of God free from their yoke of poverty, sickness, death, fear, and every unrighteousness and return all evils to sender in the mighty name of Jesus.
- I plant and build in your lives, divine favour, great grace, success, superabundance, everlasting life, everlasting joy, everlasting peace, everlasting love, every lasting prosperity,

and great anointing that breaks every yoke in the mighty name of Jesus.

- I and my family are for signs and wonders in the mighty name of Jesus I pray, amen.

6: The Heart of Man

The mind is a set of cognitive faculties that enables consciousness, perception, thinking, judgement, and memory while the heart in a literary sense is referred to as a biological organ that pumps blood repeatedly to the body and circulates the air.

It is a cognitive, reasoning, or perceptive faculty related to the process of acquiring knowledge using reasoning, intuition, or perception. In the Scriptures, we use the heart and the mind to mean the same thing which contrasts the original or dictionary meaning of the heart.

The heart is used as the mind in the Scriptures as the centre of human reasoning and processing of information both physical and spiritual. It is the command and control of your life.

Your affairs are piloted and navigated from your heart. It is also considered the gateway of emotion, imagination, success, victory, confidence, intuition, boldness, and power. "For with the heart man believeth unto righteousness, and with the mouth, confession is made unto salvation." Romans 10:10 (KJV).

The heart is the centre of life for a canal man for without it, there will not be circulation of blood and air, and without which he cannot live. For a spiritual man, apart from the normal function of the heart he must be guiding what comes in and goes out of his heart for that is very important because all issues of his life are decided in the heart.

A born-again Christian must, first, believe in his heart, the Lord Jesus Christ as his Lord and personal savior. Who came to the earth and died for us on the cross. On the third day, the Father raised Him from death. Thereafter he confesses his salvation or victory over sin and death with his mouth through the blood of the resurrected Jesus Christ. The heart is the centre of your faith and whatever you want or intend to do on earth.

Your faith, hope, and glory rely upon your heart because whatever you will do will emanate from the heart. Hence, we must put our trust in the Lord and ask Him for direction instead of relying solely on our minds. "Trust in the LORD with all thy heart and lean not unto thy understanding. In all thy ways acknowledge him, and he shall direct thy paths." Proverbs 3:5-6 (KJV).

Human wisdom and understanding are good but that which you want to do, or follow may not agree or conflict with the Word of God, particularly concerning your life. Very often people tend to go for quick fixes which they know are contrary to the Word of God which is in direct disobedience or conflict to God because they want to get out of a situation.

It could be dangerous for a person to rely upon mere human wisdom, which could look good or right in the eye of the person but the result may not be good. "There is a way that seems right to a man, but in the end, it leads to death." (Proverbs 14:12; 16:25).

The Lord says, "For my thoughts are not your thoughts, neither are your ways my ways, saith the LORD. For as the heavens are higher than the earth, so are my ways higher than your ways, and my thoughts than your thoughts." Isaiah 55:8-9 (KJV).

It all depends on your relationship with God. He is there to guide, protect and lead you in the way you should go. He is in you and works with your mind if you allow Him to be in you and work with you for you.

I have read and heard people say that God cannot tell you who to marry, what to do, or how you should live. The Lord is closer than most of us think. If the Lord has a special purpose for you, He will be always there for you even His angels because He knows you cannot do it alone on your own.

If you are going for the wrong man or woman for marriage, He will warn you, but He will not stop you. Sometimes He may not stop you from the assignment which you desire, but when problems come up,

He will remind you that He warned you. He cares about everything about us including the food that we eat or drink and the clothes that we put on. That might sound strange to some of us, but it is both fact and truth.

Leaning on the Lord for direction will help us to reduce our mistakes and not compound them, reduce our sorrows, and not compound them. No person would like to be going from one issue to the other and sometimes related issues. When He asked Abraham to leave his father's house to the land, He was going to show him, He was talking to him and directing him along the way. Your assignment is not different.

Abraham was able to exercise that level of faith that was credited to him as righteousness because the Lord was talking to him at each level of his journey. The Lord is the same yesterday, today, and forever. He is still speaking, guiding, and directing His children now as He did in the days of old. I went to a Bible study and the man of God was teaching how God guided His anointed in the time of old, and I told him that the Lord does not change and still guiding and directing His people to date.

When you give Him yourself, He will never forsake you nor leave you. He will be with you as He was with Abraham or Moses depending on the power or relationship you are having with Him.

He will move you to your promised land.

Remember when Abraham was in his father's house, he was poor, and his wife was also barren. He had nothing to show in life until the day the Lord remembered him and called him out and he obeyed. I pray to the Lord to remember you as you use this prayer book and set you on high as He did for Papa Abraham.

The Lord blessed Him and promised to make Him the Father of many nations. The irony or sarcasm of it is that some of you will not obey because you will be hearing voices and without seeing who is talking to you. Some people do not understand their emotions, hunch, or intuition when the Lord is ministering to them through their hearts or strange person or image or symbol talking to them.

Even when the three angels came to his house and he asked his wife to make food for them, some wives will not honour that wish from their husbands, particularly those of us living in London. I am now only learning that families who live in other European countries are different from those of us living in England, particularly London.

For everyone, there is a profession, calling, content, country, city, or house you can live in, and you can have positive or negative consequences in your life. Everywhere is not meant for everybody.

The environment you live in, and the association or relationship you keep will determine how far and well you can go in life. The names that you give your children and their relationships including school and college affect their lives. Working with people with a crooked mindset will affect you adversely because those spirits will be manifesting negatively in your life, and you may not understand it.

Sometimes after a short meeting say like two hours with negative people or negative mindsets, the energy you absorbed within that short time will make you look repulsive to other people should you have another meeting and then imagine the effect in your life if you are permanently living with a negative spouse or working in a team where people are of negative vibes or energy.

The Bible says do not unequally yoke with unbelievers. It is not only in marriage and business, but it could also be in any relationship in which case you have to dealing with an inferior or negative personality.

That is why we must lean completely on the Lord and allow Him to direct us. We do not need to have many struggles in life. Even as pastors, we are looking to grow our ministries quickly and work with people who we shouldn't and hold ourselves back.

The same applies to some businessmen. You keep holding yourself back and blame it on the witches, and the same applies to the job you do too. Some people are running from one pastor or church to church without learning and allowing Him to direct them.

Some people may not have a breakthrough in their church and go to another ministry to have a breakthrough and remain in the same place and lose it and go back for prayer again.

Your world is planned and constructed in your heart. Like a farmer, if you do not cultivate the land, and plant a good seed, the land will be overtaken by weeds and there will be nothing to harvest come the harvest season. A good man will plan his world well and sow good seed fit for a good harvest in his heart.

A good man is wise because he is sowing the positive things of life and shall reap goodness and his heart shall be merry.

Proverbs 17:22 says, "A merry heart doeth good like a medicine: but a broken spirit drieth the bones." A good life, success or failure is in the heart. It is how you program it to work for you that your world will be. Life is the choices we make and the way we think. At times, we walk away from opportunities and sometimes when we are being guided for our benefit, we walk away because we don't understand.

Some people succeed in their lives because they learned from their past mistakes while some don't learn or understand anything irrespective of their age and education.

You can make anything at any age or stage in life provided you do not give up and restrict yourself by thinking that you are getting much older and making amends in your life particularly the way you think and the choices you make.

The moment you have a breakthrough your attitude and appearance will change. In addition, it will change your thinking and will not only prolong your life but your lifestyle. Remember that all those trials and disappointments are not for nothing, but part of the experience and knowing that experience is the best teacher.

The Lord says, 'But if I with the finger of God cast out devils, no doubt the kingdom of God has come upon you. Luke 11:20. The way you wire your brain will determine the choices you make either to believe that the Kingdom of God is here or not. Your miracles are already here, as a man thinketh in his heart so is he. If you believe in your heart that you possess all things you have it.

Everything you need to make it in life is already in you even the Kingdom of God is not only within you but is in you until you learn to believe, you will not see even the benefits now unless you believe.

Cast out, delete, erase, wipe, and clean any negative images, utterances, pronouncements, assertions, or imaginations out of your mind so that they do not get crystallised and form part of your life. Do not allow them to hang on you because they will affect you adversely.

Now, let us look at the story surrounding Uncle Gideon when the children of Israel were in captivity and crying for help, from the Lord. The angel of the Lord went to Uncle Gideon to deliver his people. Uncle Gideon was shocked at such a request from the Lord because he did not consider himself worthy of handling such noble assignments, particularly from the Lord considering his background.

"And the angel of the LORD appeared unto him, and said unto him, The LORD is with thee, thou mighty man of valour. And Gideon said unto him, oh my Lord, if the LORD be with us, why then is all this befallen us? and where be all his miracles which our fathers told us of, saying, did not the LORD bring us up from Egypt? but now the LORD hath forsaken us, and delivered us into the hands of the Midianites.

And the LORD looked upon him, and said, go in this thy might, and thou shalt save Israel from the hand of the Midianites: have not I sent thee?

And he said unto him, oh my Lord, wherewith shall I save Israel? behold, my family is poor in Manasseh, and I am the least in my father's house. And the LORD said unto him, Surely, I will be with thee, and thou shalt smite the Midianites as one man." Judges 6:12-16(KJV).

Uncle Gideon remembered that the Lord delivered their fathers from Egyptian bondage and now allowed them to suffer the same fate in the hands of the Midianites. But when help came, he was asking for signs, and being a very merciful father, He showed him signs and promised that He was with him.

A man can go as much as the energy which is his faith can carry him. Despite that, the angel of the Lord called him a mighty man of valour, he did not believe it.

He is one of those with extraordinary grace whom the Lord will carry through with little or no faith. If you look at most of the miracles of Jesus, most of the people exhibited great faith but Uncle Gideon did not show great faith but exhibited a determination and willingness to lead in the liberation of his people. Many people cannot get to the top of the mountain because of unbelief, doubts, fear of the unknown, and what people will say.

You can make it, you can get there, and you can chase, overtake, and recover if you can only believe. All things are yours, but you do not have to go with the whole crowd because some of them may not be needed or may become distractions. Victory, success, triumph, and abundance are already in us, but impoverishment and penury are in the minds of the unbelievers.

"And the LORD said unto Gideon, the people that are with thee are too many for me to give the Midianites into their hands, lest Israel vaunt themselves against me, saying, Mine own hand hath saved me.

Now, therefore, go to proclaim in the ears of the people, saying, whosoever is fearful and afraid, let him return and depart early from Mount Gilead. And there returned of the people twenty and two thousand, and there remained ten thousand.

And the LORD said unto Gideon, The people are yet too many; bring them down unto the water, and I will try them for thee there: and it shall be, that of whom I say unto thee, This shall go with thee, the same shall go with thee; and of whomsoever I say unto thee, This shall not go with thee, the same shall not go.

So, he brought down the people unto the water: and the LORD said unto Gideon, everyone that lappeth of the water with his tongue, as a dog lappeth, him shalt thou set by himself; likewise, everyone that bowed down upon his knees to drink.

And the number of them that lapped, putting their hand to their mouth, were three hundred men: but all the rest of the people bowed down upon their knees to drink water. And the LORD said unto Gideon, By the three hundred men that lapped will I save you and deliver the Midianites into thine hand: and let all the other people go every man unto his place." Judges 7:2-7 (KJV).

Believe in the Lord and lean unto Him because He can do exceedingly and abundantly above our expectations and imaginations. This world is a war zone, and we are getting through every day because the Lord is fighting for us without us seeing what is going on, for we war not against flesh and blood but against principalities and powers and spiritual darkness in high places.

It does not matter how many battalions are against us, you can be assured that those who care for us are more than the enemies. We don't need too many people, particularly the unbelievers, fearful, distractors, and saboteurs.

If Christ is for us, who can be against us? Praise God. "Then Gideon took ten men of his servants and did as the LORD had said unto him: and so, it was, because he feared his father's household, and the men of the city, that he could not do it by day, that he did it by night.

And when the men of the city arose early in the morning, behold, the altar of Baal was cast down, and the grove was cut down that was by it, and the second bullock was offered upon the altar that was built. And they said one to another, who hath done this thing? And when they enquired and asked, they said, Gideon, the son of Joash hath done this thing." Judges 6:27-29(KJV).

It is a norm that the foundation must be on solid ground, otherwise, it will be cracked, fallen, and destroyed. The spirit must be renewed for the anointing to break the yoke or be broken.

Mental toughness is required, and attitudes and thinking must be changed to conform to a belief system acceptable to the Lord.

That is why the Lord ordered Uncle Gideon to go and destroy all the Baal temples and build a temple for the Lord God of Host. Jesus says, "And no man putteth new wine into old bottles; else the new wine will burst the bottles, and be spilt, and the bottles shall perish. But new wine must be put into new bottles, and both are preserved." (Matthew 9:17).

Sacrifices were made unto the Lord and every evil or negative imagination was cast down to the glory of God. True victory comes with true beliefs and mindsets which is true thinking hence you cannot have new wine in old bottles. Anything that tries to exalt itself against the knowledge of God must be brought to the obedience of the Word of God which is that Christ in you.

All things created by God are spiritual even heaven and the earth are spirit beings, and the understanding of spiritual laws is crucial to appreciating how spiritual things work. Location, time or season, and the people you are dealing with or working with are very important in your victory or success. It's just as important to believe and speaking the truth as to have your daily bread.

When you learn the Word of God and meditate on it, you should be able to hear from God directly and through His angels or revelation in your dreams and open visions, for where there is no vision the people perish. He is not usually far from those who are seeking Him.

From time to time, He will speak to you, and you will hear Him clearly and know that it is Him who is speaking to you, particularly when you allow Him to take charge of the business of your life for you.

That does not mean that He will not allow you to go through the fire or the waters but when you are going through them, He will be with you and give you all the necessary encouragement and make escape routes for you. Tests and challenges are part of life and without them, there will be no testimonies. 'In everything give thanks: for this is the will of God in Christ Jesus concerning you.' 1 Thessalonians 5:18 (KJV).

If anything comes your way and the Lord disallows it, it will not proceed. However, sometimes He will allow you to be tested depending on the level of lifting or promotion on the way, your faith may be tested and sometimes very seriously. Depending on the grace in your life, He will inform you well in advance before the events.

The Psalmist wrote 'The Lord hath chastened me sore but He hath not given me over unto death.' He knew it was the Lord because He told him. King Solomon wrote in the book of Proverbs that 'He chastises those He loves.' Chastisement is a process that everyone passes through. He prepares you to become strong and fit for the work you are going to do. In other words, fit for your purpose. "For whom the LORD loveth he corrects; even as a father the son in whom he delights." Proverbs 3:12 (KJV).

If you are one of those called into the deliverance and healing ministry, then you will be expected to go through a tougher regime and after that, you will never be the same again. You do not try to do things your way. When you allow Him all the way, you will see little, or no mistakes and you will never be the same anymore. You will see many more things and deal with situations in a way you couldn't ordinarily deal with on your own.

Man's heart is necessary for shaping his future and as a result, it is necessary to have a good Spirit working in the heart with a positive mental attitude to life. The life of a man is basically what he thinks in his heart and what he wants to make of it, success, or failure.

If you believe in your heart that you will serve the Lord our God and walk in His ways, so you shall. If one adopts a negative attitude, he will hold himself back and go on to think that the evil ones are after him. You are successful when you believe it, think about it, speak about success and work on it. It is all in the mind or belief system or faith.

"A good man out of the good treasures of his heart bringeth forth that which is good, and an evil man out of the evil treasure of his heart bringeth forth that which is evil: from the abundance of the heart his mouth speaks." Luke 6:45 (KJV). No good fruit could come out of a bad tree, neither can a bad fruit come out of a good tree.

Of course, some good fruits may become worse when they are overripe or decay or eaten by some animals or inserts. Each tree will yield fruit and seed according to its kind and the Word of God can as well change those bad fruits. In the same way, a born-again can drift away from the truth with the pleasures of this life when he gets himself involved with bad companies or associations. The Bible warns that bad associations destroy useful habits.

Watching corrupt television programmes, and films and reading bad books can cause a Christian to stumble. That is why the Bible warns us of involvement with unbelievers, particularly in marriage and other associations.

In the same manner, a good man will think of victory, triumph, success, blessing, overcoming, love, peace, conquering, and reigning and confess the same with his mouth and put them into practice. That's because that is the abundance in his heart.

But a foolish or negative man will conceive all negative things in his heart, speak and practice them and blame witches or evil people, when in fact he is responsible for the problems. Some go as far as sleeping with married women which is the biggest curse and causing disaffection among brethren.

Proverbs 10:11 says, 'The mouth of a righteous man is a well of life: but violence covers the mouth of the wicked.' A man believes in his heart and confesses with his mouth. A good man speaks life while a wicked or foolish man heaps curses on himself, sometimes as jokes or out of ignorance and they work against him.

When a person is speaking out of ignorance with negative words to himself and those around him, he is heaping curses. Some of them call themselves comedians. Please reject that in your life and that of your children and children's, children.

It is what is in the heart of a man that he shall speak or do. It is the spirit that dwells in the heart that determines what the person will be and do. If the Holy Spirit dwells in your heart, then you will have the mindset of Christ and you will think and speak like Him.

"These things we also speak, not in words which man's wisdom teaches but which the Holy Spirit teaches, comparing spiritual things with spiritual. But the natural man does not receive the things of the Spirit of God, for they are foolishness to him; nor can he know them because they are spiritually discerned.

But he who is spiritual judges all things, yet he is rightly judged by no one. For 'who has known the mind of the LORD that he may instruct Him?' But we have the mind of Christ." 1 Corinthians 2:13-16 (KJV).

Spiritual things are designed or meant for those who are spiritually discerned and are foolish to an ordinary or carnal man for they will not make sense to him because they are not discerned to understand the secrets of the Kingdom.

Christ never spoke negative things which may be the fact, but He spoke in parables and the truth. For it is only the truth that will make us free. I have this friend who complains about not being well to attract sympathy and I continue to warn him about his utterances. One day he walked up and said to me, "If I can only speak 'it is well' as you continue to warn me, then I shall be well."

Of course, he became well as soon as his mindset was reconditioned that he is well having prayed for him because it is in the mind. Again, I have this lady friend who was going through eviction and came in casually for counselling and I told her that the Lord is with her and will make a way for her.

Thereafter, she continued to moan, and I continued to warn her. She came in a few days later with a big smile on her face, and I asked her what the catch was, and she said, "Immediately you prayed for me, and I began to think and confess 'it is well' everything became well." Keeping your property and losing it is in your mind and what you agree with your God.

It does not mean that you are not going to pay your debt but may receive more time to pay, or a further source of income. However, you may also have some more serious miracle or grace in which case your debts can be written off or receive someone to help. Praise God!

Prayer:

- Lord, I pray for an understanding heart like that of King Solomon.

- Let Thy great grace guide us like in the day of Pentecost;

- Every open door that the enemies are using as a snare or entrap us be shut and sealed forthwith in Jesus' mighty name.

- Oh Lord, guide my heart with thy all diligence; for out of it are the issues of my life, in Jesus' mighty name I pray, amen.

- IT IS WELL WITH MY SOUL IN THE NAME OF JESUS!!!

7: The Power in the Blood of Jesus

Very often we use the blood and the name of our Lord Jesus without adequately relating or equating them to the power, rights, and privileges that go with them. First, let us look at the meaning of 'power!' Power is the ability or authority to execute or perform an act.

Ability to do what? Someone may ask. In politics and social sciences, power is the ability to influence others. Sometimes, we associate it with influence, strength, might, energy, or authority.

In economics, we look at purchasing power, economic power, monopoly power, class power, bargaining power, etc.

A rich man who has economic power can influence his community, even the market depending on how rich he is and the distribution of wealth in his community. I do not wish to go too much into the worldly power definitions or explanations but I'm only trying to use it to get you to the understanding of the word 'power.'

Blood is something very sacred or holy and it is life on its own. It is special and special to the Creator. Jesus is a Lamb of God without blemish. It is only His blood that is perfect and sufficient for our sanctification. It is only the blood that has the power of sanctification, purification, cleansing and justification. It is used for atonement for our sins so that we are forgiven and become the righteousness of God through Him who was righteous and made sin.

Leviticus 17:11 says, "For the life of the flesh is in the blood, and I have given it to you upon the altar to make atonement for your souls; for it is the blood that makes atonement for the soul." You know that your life is in your blood and without this blood, there is no life in you. This is more than extraordinary blood without blemish of a man who knew no sin.

Blood is the life in the flesh, and it is only pure and unblemished blood that can be used for sanctification and redemption of the world once and for all times. You are born of God and not of flesh and blood because of the shedding and pouring out of the holy blood of the Lamb of God to reconcile us to the Father. The shedding of the blood of the Lamb is the ministry of reconciliation of the Lord Jesus by reconciling the world to the Father.

"Which were born, not of blood, nor of the will of the flesh, nor the will of man, but of God. And the Word was made flesh and dwelt among us, (and we beheld his glory, the glory as of the only begotten of the Father,) full of grace and truth." John 1:13-14 (KJV).

We believe and declare the power in the blood of our Lord Jesus Christ but often we do not know the degree of the power in the blood of Jesus.

"In Him, we have redemption through His blood, the forgiveness of sins, according to the riches of His grace which He made to abound toward us in all wisdom and prudence." Ephesians1:7-8 (NKJV).

In the blood of the Lamb, we have our redemption. That is, we were bought back, traded in our sins, and converted into new creatures. His blood is used to make amends for our sins and redress and justify us.

It is the atonement that has been done once and cannot be repeated. It is once for all times and if you know the power and privileges that go with it, you will turn back and ask God why He has favoured you this way or so much.

His blood is the blood that gave us salvation, and deliverance, or rescued us from the power of sin and death. Without this blood of the Lamb, there is nothing anyone could have done to bring us back to the Father. "For he hath made him sin for us, who knew no sin; that we might be made the righteousness of God in him." 2 Corinthians 5:2 (KJV).

The Father gave His Son the ministry of reconciliation in which case He reconciled men to the Father through Himself by giving up His own life.

Reconciliation or deliverance means that we no longer have sinned but become like the Father, and no power or principality can hold us captive or stand in our way. You are incorruptible when you become like the Father and think and speak like Him.

A redeemed son of God is completely redeemed or delivered from the consequences of sin and death, and you become totally like your Father without blemish. As the gate of hell was not able to prevail over Christ, it will be impossible for sin, sickness, or death to hold us captive because we have overcome them with the blood of the lamb and the words of our testimonies.

"And almost all things are by the law purged with blood, and without shedding of blood is no remission." Hebrews 9:22 (KJV).

By law atonement and remission of sins were made with the blood of any animal which could be a clean goat, sheep, or bird, and without such sacrifice, no forgiveness or reduction of sin was possible. Although His grace abides forever, that procedure was followed under the law for the remission of sins to take place.

The blood was not only used for the cleansing or forgiveness of sins, but it was also used to protect the child of God from diseases and attacks even from the enemies. At that time, the crime or sin must be balanced with the sacrificial lamb which must be killed for purification to take place or for protection to take place.

In this case, there is no equation or something to be compared to the power or authority in the blood of the Son of God who is perfect and a worthy lamb to purify the sins of the world. For it pleased the Lord to use the blood of His only begotten to rescue the world and reconcile us to Himself as He gave Him the ministry of reconciliation. Praise God!

"And thus, shall ye eat it; with your loins girded, your shoes on your feet, and your staff in your hand; and ye shall eat it in haste: it is the LORD'S Passover. For I will pass through the land of Egypt this night and will smite all the firstborn in the land of Egypt, both man and beast; and against all the gods of Egypt I will execute judgement: I am the LORD.

And the blood shall be to you for a token upon the houses where you are: and when I see the blood, I will Passover you and the plague shall not come upon you to destroy you when I smite the land of Egypt.'" Exodus 12:11-13 (KJV).

The power in the blood is triggered as soon as the blood is ministered. When you minister the blood be ready for the action because it moves with the anointing of the Lord to effect salvation or deliverance and every yoke shall be destroyed.

The children of Israel were in bondage in the land of Egypt for several years, and at that time they were crying to the Lord to deliver them from such bondage.

The Lord appeared to Moses and appointed him a leader so that he could lead the children of God to the land He had promised their ancestor Abraham. Moses was sceptical as to whether Pharaoh and his people, as well as the children of Israel, would believe him.

He asked for signs and the Lord told him what to do and as Pharaoh continued to disobey, the Lord hardened his heart the more, and He continued to send plagues in the land of Egypt.

For the fact that you are sanctified with the blood of Jesus, any evil that tries to come against you, the Holy Spirit will see them before they can do anything and send a plague on them so that they will not be able to perform their devilish acts. Sometimes the Lord hardens the hearts of your enemies so they will not stop, and He sends more plagues to them. Praise God!

It came to pass that the Lord decided to smite all firstborns in the land of Egypt both man and beasts. He commanded the Hebrews to get a one-year-old lamb from their sheep or goat and the lamb must be unblemished and free from any disease or defects according to the needs of the family.

If the family is too small to finish the lamb, they should join with their nearest neighbours.

He commanded that they should kill a lamb and sprinkle the blood on the two doorposts of their houses so that when the angel of death visits the land of Egypt to slay all the firstborn both man and beasts, it shall not affect them. When the angel of death sees the blood on their doorposts, they shall pass over the house.

Here, the blood of the lamb in this situation was not used to cleanse or for purification but used as a shield or cover.

As the original unblemished Lamb of God had not arrived, it was necessary to use the blood of the makeshift or improvised lamb for the deliverance of the children of Israel from the land of Egypt.

"For we know in part, and we prophesy in part. But when that which is perfect has come, then that which is in part shall be done away." I Corinthians 13:9-10 (KJV).

By law, the blood of the lamb either goat or sheep was shed for atonement or remission of sins and protection as in the Passover. For every need of remission, atonement, and shield, separate sacrificial blood had to be shed. It was done in part for each one according to his own needs.

Now He that is perfect, the Lord Jesus Christ has arrived, the atonement was done for the whole world and no more in part or on individual bases. It was made for all people and for all times to all that believe.

The priests were then making the same sacrifices daily which in truth were not able to take away sins (see Hebrews 10:11). Now that our Lord Jesus Christ who is perfect is with us, those things have been done away with.

As the blood of our Lord has been poured out for us at the Calvary, that which was in part had been done away with because the priests do not have to make the same sacrifices every day.

Although, the blood of the ordinary lamb had not the power and force of complete atonement, remission of sins to protect us from the fairy darts of the enemies.

"For one offering he hath perfected forever them that are sanctified." Hebrews 10:14 (KJV).

For this sacrifice, He who knew no sin was made sin for us so that we might become the righteousness of God through Him who gave up His life for us.

It was done once and for all time so that whosoever that believeth in Him shall have victory over all the powers of the enemies including death which has been swallowed in victory.

The Lord told the children of Israel at the Passover to kill and sprinkle the blood of the lamb on their doorposts, roast and eat it in haste and ready to go. The blood of our Lord has been provided for us and is available to use at any time. When going to bed at night, simply pray and use the blood of Jesus to cover your family, yourself, your house, everything, and everywhere that matters to you and you will find out that the enemies cannot come near because you are sanctified.

Those things and places you mentioned are fully covered or protected with the blood of Jesus Christ our Lord. Follow the same routine every morning and do the same day in and day out and you will find out that you have victory over the witches and all the powers of the enemies.

When you pray and cover your finances, assets, businesses, children, relatives, and neighbours with the blood, you will certainly see the difference because the sun shall not smite them by day nor the moon by night. No plague, witchcraft, or enemies shall be able to go near them but shall pass over them because of the blood of the new covenant.

Speak it as often as you can and those for whom it was spoken on their behalf shall be blessed or sanctified with it and all the plans, arrows, and fairy darts of the enemies shall pass over them as in the day of Passover in Egypt and nothing shall harm or hurt them.

"But Christ being come a high priest of good things to come, by a greater and more perfect tabernacle, not made with hands, that is to say, not of this building; Neither by the blood of goats and calves, but by his own blood he entered in once into the holy place, having obtained eternal redemption for us." Hebrews 9:11-12 (KJV).

The King came as a high priest of good things, signifying the good nature and abundant life promised in God's kingdom where there will be no pains, hunger, sickness, and death.

A mirror that we can use to see life from a different perspective or angle. Our Lord came down as a High Priest and offered sacrifice for us for the cleansing and purification of our sins once and for all times and it is a sign or symbol of greater and more perfect things to come to us.

To wit, trampling on snakes and serpents and scorpions and destroying all the powers of the enemies and nothing shall by any means hurt us. Christ the King is Lord over all situations and powers and principalities. At the sight of you or me, they tremble because He is dwelling in us.

"Far above all principality, and power, and might, and dominion, and every name that is named, not only in this world but also in that which is to come." Ephesians 1:21 (KJV).

Witches and blood-sucking demons cause sudden and untimely deaths through road accidents. This can be avoided with prayer and asking for journey mercies with the blood of Jesus.

The blood will give you protection and victory over the powers of the enemies because when they see the blood they must pass over. After all, that is the laid down rule from the Lord. This is the truth that will make us free. Praise God!

"For where there is a [last] will and testament involved, the death of the one who made it must be established." Hebrews 9:16 (AMP).

In real-life situations, will and testaments cannot be implemented except when the death of the one who made the will has been established. Christ is alive and His will and testaments are being implemented because all powers and authorities both in heaven and on earth have been given to Him and at the mention of that name, 'Jesus' every knee must bow, and every tongue must confess that He is Lord.

Some people are above the laws of the land but very few people like King Charles III of the United Kingdom is above the laws of the land.

Christ the King is the only person who is above all laws. He is the only person who can break the laws of hell and the grave. He went to hell and took the keys and came out.

He despised the grave as it could not hold him captive because He conquered death. The laws of gravity could not apply to him, because He is the only thing and person who went up and did not come down.

"That in (at) the name of Jesus every knee should (must) bow, in heaven and on earth and under the earth, and every tongue [frankly and openly] confess and acknowledge that Jesus Christ is Lord, to the Glory of God the Father." Philippians 2:10-11(AMP).

"Then I heard a loud voice saying in heaven, now is the salvation, and strength, and the kingdom of our God, and the power of His Christ have come, for the accuser of our brethren, who accused them before our God, day, and night, has been cast down. And they overcame him by the blood of the Lamb and by the word of their testimony, and they did not love their lives to the death." Revelation 12:10-11.

When the blood of the Lord came down and touched the ground and He gave up the ghost, He said that 'it is finished.' As He gave up the ghost, darkness took over the day because the blood of a perfect Priest had been shed through false accusation,

Those who accused our brethren day and night were immediately driven down from heaven because the blood of the righteous King has been shed to cleanse the heaven and the earth from all unrighteousness.

It pleased the Lord for Christ to die the shameful and painful death for us so that we do not have to go through the same again and have life and have it more abundantly. However, if anyone has to go through the same, He will know and understand because He is acquainted with pain and sorrow and the consequences of envy when people are pointing accusing fingers at an innocent person.

In this case, His blood will speak more for you even when you are on the sick bed, the strips He took for your sake will speak more for you to come back to life. Praise God!

Even as we speak now, He is acquainted with everything you are seeing or hearing to come to your aide.

The evils cannot come near the blood because the purified and sanctified blood of the Lamb consumes them with burning flames of fire and strikes them with thunder before they get near and burst into flames. I pray that the Lord will open your eyes so that you can see how the Blood deals with the kingdom of darkness when you keep up with your confession of the Blood.

Praise God and shout aloud:

- I overcome them with the blood of Jesus and the words of my testimonies!

- The blood of the lamb has been shed for me once and for all times!
- I am the victorious one! Hallelujah!

8: Destroying the Power of the Witches

Some of us take this topic of the witches for granted because they have not experienced or encountered it in their lives or encountered it without knowing why they are the way they are.

You are born to excel, you are born to prosper, you are born to win, you are born to conquer, you are born to succeed, you are born to reign and not a slave, failure, or loser.

Why is your life stagnant, neither moving forward nor backward, nor sometimes instead of going forward, they keep going backward, shrinking, or standing still?

Do you think, do you ask questions, do you read books or listen to specialists in the field? I came from an environment where people do not see the light.

When you raise your head, they kill you off, if they cannot kill you, they try to frustrate, suffocate, or strangulate your life. Some can monitor your life with ordinary water in a bowl or mirror in any part of the world, no matter who or where you are. You can call it magic or anything, I know is spiritual and it is the spiritual realm that controls the physical.

They monitor you as soon as you are born. If you are not within the environment and live outside the community and perhaps abroad and planning a project, you must be very careful. If you have what it takes to complete your project, do it quickly otherwise they will frustrate it. Many people are living frustrated and unaccomplished lives without knowing why their lives are going that way while some others are living fulfilling lives.

You must find out whether the evil ones are after you or if you are holding yourself with an evil, negative mental attitude, or mindset. Evil thoughts and negative mindsets work in the same manner as witchcraft.

Those wicked people do not see any progress in their lives, even their children and children's children. The devil has blinded their mind, and they cannot think and see. They fail to see that they are not only stopping others but their families and their generations following.

The Lord promised to visit up to four generations for the iniquities of their fathers (Deuteronomy 5:9). Most of them go to church and worship idols and think like the idols which they are serving.

An idol mind cannot think of anything good but idol-evil service. The Bible says, "Suffer not the witches to live" (Exodus 22:18). God does not condone evil. He hates it and does not want us to partake in that evil or suffer from it.

The Cambridge Dictionary defines witchcraft as "the activity of performing magic to help or harm other people." It sounds so simple if you do not understand the gravity of witchcraft. My question is, why should somebody sit down and think about how to harm his neighbour? Again, why would you want to help a person harm another instead of trying to settle their differences? Isn't that madness or crazy?

Some people do not believe in witchcraft. It is good if you do not believe in them, and you are very good at praying. If you do not believe in them and do not pray, you are leaving yourself to be swallowed up by them when they remember you. They do not bewitch every person but those they envy or consider a threat. The symptoms of witchcraft are like that of curses and let us look at some of them:

Some symptoms of witchcraft:

- A brilliant student is not able to pass examinations, whereas the less brilliant ones are passing the same exam. This is the work of destiny killers.
- Difficulty getting into higher education or apprenticeship while others with a similar background are getting them. The work of destiny killers.
- Problems getting a job after education or training. The work of destiny killers.
- Having problems in your business or job while others in the same field or occupation are thriving while you are at a standstill. The work of the dream killers.
- When the children are so delinquent and are not able to do or understand anything. The work of envious relatives.
- Where you have many children in the family and they are not able to get married, particularly the girls. Handwork of the enemies.
- A situation where a person works or does business and is always broke when in fact, he is making money. Devouring spirit, work of the enemies.
- Where a skilled person cannot get a job, or he is in business, and nothing works. Work of the destiny killers.
- When a person gets sick or unwell when is the time to go to an interview or exams? Work of dream killers.
- Sudden or untimely death through accidents or some other useless viruses. Work of the enemies.
- Miscarriages and delays in conceptions. Work of the enemies,
- Late marriages particularly among men. Work of the enemies.

- Walking or tracking endlessly in the dreams even in the bush and sometimes you miss your way, typical witchcraft.
- Being unable to coordinate what you are doing and planning well your life, is the work of evil people.
- Children dying young. Work of the enemies.
- Confusion, delays, and going in circles in life. Work of the enemies.
- No promotion in life even at work. Work of the enemies.
- No favour. Work of the enemies.
- You cannot go to church to seek solutions. Work of the enemies.
- Attacks in your dream.

You may ask why they are doing this to you and what have you done to deserve this. You do not have to do anything to them. It is in their nature to be wicked and do evil. It is not that they cannot change, they can repent and change.

Most of them are driven by jealousy and envy, whereas, in some people, it is their nature. They do not want to see anything good in anybody. "These wicked people are born sinners; even from birth they have lied and gone their own way. "Psalm 58:3 (NLT).

They go astray as soon as they are born telling lies about those, they are bewitching saying that they do not want to marry, they cannot have children, they do not want to work, they do not want to go to school or college.

They do not want this; they do not want that when in fact what they are doing is spreading the news of their witchcraft so that people will hate and despise you. "A lying tongue hated those that are afflicted by it; and a flattering mouth worketh ruin." Proverbs 26:28 (KJV).

They will sow so much discord in your life that even when you get to understand the source of your predicament, you will have nobody to talk to or turn to because they have already blackmailed you. They think that they can get away with such evil; of course, they cannot because their shame shall shame them because whatever a man sows, he shall reap.

Now you may ask again, who could be doing this to me? It can be anybody who is jealous of you or has an evil mind against you and any person threatened by your presence. John 10:10 says, "The thief cometh not, but for to steal, and to kill, and to destroy, I have come that they might have life and that they might have it more abundantly."

These people are agents of Satan, and their mission is just to steal, kill and destroy. They are happy to accomplish their evil mandates and see others crying.

They could be your relatives particularly, the uncles and aunties. These are people that you helped to pay their hospital bills, buy things for their families, and pay school fees for their children. Give your hard-earned money. Mind you, they do not use most of the money or things which you gave to them, for themselves but use them for witchcraft as a contact point to kill or harm you and your family. Some mothers-in-laws are not exonerated but fathers-in-law hardly had time for this type of nonsense except those who are witches by nature.

Some brothers and sisters do it also, particularly when the brothers start getting their own families, things will not continue the way they were. Particularly when a wicked woman is married into the home or family. Marriage is another one, be very careful as some husbands or wives are using their partners for rituals even their children.

I saw an interview on YouTube where a young man chased his suffering mother out and his fiancé refused, he chased both of them out stating that when the money stopped coming, she (the fiancé) would also leave, meaning that the suffering and pains of his mother yields wealth for him. He was defending his shameful action by calling his mother names, God forbid.

The Bible says, 'Money is the root of all evils.' Most of them are not wicked to you because of money, but to frustrate you and keep you low to rule or reign over you. Even some spouses do this to their husband or wife so that they can have free hands to do whatever they like.

Finally, the type of friends we keep. Most of the people that smile at your face may be hiding things in their minds. The Bible says, 'It is not all that calls me Lord, Lord, that will get into the Kingdom of the Father.' Meaning that it is not all that calls you a friend that loves you (Matthew 7:21).

"Draw me not away with the wicked, and with the workers of iniquity, which speak peace to their neighbours, but mischief is in their hearts.

Give them according to their deeds, and according to the wickedness of their endeavours: give them after the work of their hands; render to them their desert." Psalm 28:3-4 (KJV). We need to be very careful and prayerful. If you are one of those who get visions or revelations, when the Holy Spirit reveals them to you, you may not believe them because it may be someone whom you so love and respect. Therefore, it shall come as a surprise to you.

Know that the Spirit of God searches all things and lets us know whatever He wants to know. Of course, He will not reveal those things to you if you are not in tune with Him.

"But as it is written, Eye hath not seen, nor ear heard, neither have entered into the heart of man, the things which God hath prepared for them that love him. But God hath revealed them unto us by his Spirit: for the Spirit searches all things, yea, the deep things of God.

For what man knoweth the things of a man, save the spirit of man which is in him? Even so, the things of God knoweth no man, but the Spirit of God." I Corinthians 2:9-11 (KJV). I pray that the Lord will open the eyes of your mind to see and your spiritual mind to understand. Now we are going to take some prayers which you can tailor to your own specific needs.

Our Lord is the head of all powers and principalities, and He has authority over them. "And ye are complete in him, which is the head of all principality and power:" Colossians 2:10) (KJV).

He is in you; you also have authority over them. All those powers of witchcraft cannot work if you bind them. Meaning that whatever has been refused in heaven has also been refused on earth.

Witchcraft cannot work in heaven and should not work on children of God on earth because we are heavenly citizens. They manipulate the children of God through fear and lack of knowledge.

Matthew 18:18 says, "Assuredly, I say to you, whatever you bind on earth will be bound in heaven, and whatever you loose on earth will be loosed in heaven." As we believe in our hearts, let us confess with our mouths. Let us pray:

- Lord, Your Word says, "whatsoever is bound on earth is bound in heaven and whatsoever is loosed in heaven is loosed on earth."
- In the name of Jesus Christ of Nazareth, a name above all names, I bind all witchcraft spirits after my life and that of my family.

- I bind them and they remain bound and Holy Ghost fire consumes them now including their sources and foundation, as many that gather and agree with them including their chief priests.
- Holy Ghost fire consumes them and whosoever is mentioning our names for evil and their evil altars and shrines.
- Let them burn to ashes and let not their ashes turn to beauty.
- Lord, execute judgement against them and their gods.
- Let those who are working against our destiny, destroy their own instead.
- I lose our blessings; Lord kindly open the windows of the heavens and shower us with your numerous superabundant blessings.
- I lose our freedom, our marriage, our children, our finances, our jobs/businesses, our joy, our peace, and victory.
- I lose our good health, children and prosperity to locate us now.
- Thank You Lord for answering us in Jesus' mighty name, I pray. Amen.

9: Evil Plans Cannot Stand

Witchcraft is one of the weapons of the enemies to distract attention and ruin lives. The Lord who gave them the power to make such weapons did not ask them to use them against us and if they do, it shall not work.

Everyone has a calling on the face of the earth. For us to fulfil such a calling, the Lord has equipped us for that.

That's why you have many professions and even men of God with different callings or anointing. The powers came from the Lord to do good works even to heal but the people decided to use them for evil. If you look at the dictionary definition of witchcraft, it is the ability or power to propel a person to success or to harm a person.

When you revise the power to bring life, it will bring death and that is exactly what they are doing with witchcraft. Those harming people with witchcraft are supposed to use them to bless their victims.

"No weapon that is formed against thee shall prosper, and every tongue that shall rise against thee in judgement thou shalt condemn. This is the heritage of the servants of the Lord, and their righteousness is of me, saith the Lord." Isaiah 54:17 (KJV).

Not only that they shall not prosper, but Isaiah 7:7 also says, "Thus saith the Lord God, it shall not stand, neither shall it come to pass." It does not matter what they think or do, they cannot overcome us.

The Lord designed this world in a way that there must be both light and darkness, evil and good according to your choice. But

He will not allow evil to overcome good and darkness to overcome the light.

They can only do you any harm when you allow fear to overshadow your faith. It is our right as children of God that no weapon that is fashioned against us shall prosper.

They shall be returned to the senders in Jesus' name. We were dead and raised with Christ and that Spirit which raised Him from death is in us and quickens everything about us.

Therefore, greater is He that is in us than he that is in the world. If Christ is in you, who can be against you? No weapon formed against you shall prosper.

Now say this prayer:

- Oh! Jehovah God of the host, who have covered our heads in the day of battle, grant not Oh Lord the desires of the wicked, further not their wicked devices else, they exalt themselves.
- As for the head of those that compass us about, let the mischiefs of their own heart cover them.
- Let their evil fall upon them.
- Let them go down into the pit which they have dug for us.
- Let their feet be caught in the net which they have hidden for us.
- Into that very destruction let them fall and our soul shall be joyful in the Lord and say who is like unto Thee who deliver the poor from him that too strong for him.
- No weapon whatsoever that is fashioned against us shall prosper in Jesus' mighty name I pray. Amen.

10: Targeted Prayers

Now we are going to take some short, and targeted prayers.

They Shall Come to Nought

Know that the witches, do not have any other work to do but to invoke their evil spirits. The only way of stopping them is by praying without ceasing and not stopping.

It does not matter how much counsel they take; we are more than able for the Lord is with us.

"Take counsel together, and it shall come to nought; speak the word, and it shall not stand for God is with us." Isaiah 8:10 (KJV).

Wherever they gather to do their incantations and call our names for evil, it will not stand, nor will they come to pass.

Let us pray:

- Lord as they gather to take counsel against us, let their counsel turn to foolishness like Ahithophel.
- Lord as they gather for evil, let their evil fall upon them.
- Let them use their evil and wickedness against themselves.
- Their evil counsel shall not work against us and shall come to nought.
- As many as gathered, as many that took counsel together, as many as imagined or meditated, let their evils fall upon them and never depart from them unless they repent and make good of any evil or mischief they have done.

- Their evils shall not stand unto us, neither shall they come to pass in the mighty name of Jesus, we pray. Amen.
- Let the enemies turn their swords against each other in Jesus's name, amen.
- Oh Lord, let thy loving kindness and tender mercies continually preserve us now and forever in the mighty name of Jesus, I pray, amen.

Prayer Against Evil Devices

"Rest in the Lord and wait patiently for him: fret not thyself because of him who prospered in his way, because of the man who bringeth wicked devices to pass. Cease from anger and forsake wrath: fret not thyself in any wise to do evil." Psalm 37:7-8 (KJV).

The evil people do not care about other people but continue their enterprise of witchcraft. They do not care about the injuries and pains they are causing people and insist on their wickedness. Nonetheless, you should not be like them for whatever a man sows he shall reap.

"The wicked in his pride doth persecute the poor: let them be taken in the devices that they have imagined." Psalms 10:2 (KJV).

We are going to pray to send back all wickedness to the senders. Wickedness is not usually applied the moment the spell, hex, or witchcraft is cast on the victim but the time it was planned or imagined in the mind of the perpetrators. Every enterprise of the man comes from the heart. He will first plan it and think of it before executing it.

Now let us pray:

- Lord do not allow the enemies to overcome us.

- Let them be taken in the devices that they have imagined.
- Let the wickedness of their own heart fall upon them.
- Let them fall into the pit they have made and let the net they have hidden catch them.
- Into that their destruction, let them fall.
- Thank You, Lord, for making ways for us where there was no way and blessing us beyond curses.
- Thank You, Lord, for defending us in the mighty name of Jesus we pray. Amen.

Prayer Against Fastened Nails

Some evil priests use their evil shrines or altars to cage people or hold them in bondage. In those places, they are always making incantations against the children of God for evil.

Most of the time it was not your fault, only because some persons had taken your name there out of envy and gave them some money to kill or hold you back from achieving your destiny or goals.

In these cases, they will use your picture, money, hair, clothes, or anything from you as a contact point and nail or tie with rope or both. Some of them will nail to the wall, tree, and ground, and in such places, they consider appropriate for their evil work.

Some may drop them in their evil shrine, some into the river or seas, bury them in the ground or under the ground, nail them to a tree, and sometimes outside the planet Earth. While some may lock the person in a bottle, other containers and some will chain, tie with cords, or rope, or any other means they consider appropriate.

"In that day, saith the Lord of hosts, shall the nail that is fastened in the sure place be removed, and be cut down, and fall; and the burden that was upon it shall be cut off: for the Lord hath spoken it." Isaiah 22:25 (KJV). The mouth of the Lord has spoken it.

Now declare the prayer below and those captivities shall be taken captive:

- I decree and declare that the nails fastened in sure places against me, be removed now and the sure places are cut down now in Jesus' name.
- Any sure places, or evil altars where they have taken our names, family names for whatever reason receive ministerial fire and let them be burnt to ashes while we are set free from their demonic agenda in the mighty name of Jesus.
- Let the Holy Ghost fire descend and consume all their evil altars and shrines with their high priests and agents now in Jesus' name.
- Let their mischiefs fall upon them in Jesus' name. Amen.
- Let those trees where those nails are fastened be consumed by the fire of the Holy Ghost forthwith as the fire consumes the woods in Jesus' mighty name. Amen.
- Let the walls where these nails are fastened come down forthwith like the wall of Jericho in the mighty name of Jesus. Amen.
- I decree; and declare that you lose your hosts now in Jesus' name. Amen.
- Lose him and let him go now.
- Lose him and let him go now.
- Lose him and let him go now.
- Thank You, Lord, for setting us free in Jesus' name.
- We worship You, Lord, for answered prayers in Jesus' mighty name we pray. Amen.

Trample on Snakes and Scorpions

Our Father says, "My people are destroyed for lack of knowledge." Hosia 4:6. We go through many things on earth today because we have decided to follow our ways and do our things in our way.

Every power or authority is in our hands to rule the earth and manage it according to the Father's plan or will for us. Often people miss out and suffer because they fail to realise that greater is He that is in us than he that is in the world.

"And it shall come to pass afterwards, that I will pour out my spirit upon all flesh; and your sons and your daughters shall prophesy, your old men shall dream dreams, your young men shall see visions." Joel 2:28 (KJV).

We can see the power of God on earth now as never before because of the outpouring of the Holy Spirit. There are more healings now than in the days of Christ on earth, more prosperity, visions, and wisdom.

This outpouring of the Spirit is not confined to a set of people but all flesh. For as many that believe shall be called sons of God. All those who believe shall receive it.

This prophecy did not end in just the power of vision among the churches, but great miracles, signs, and wonders are following the children of God in many churches including healings and deliverances. Of course, it works for those who believe. It is of faith, a belief system, or a mindset.

You cannot walk on snakes and scorpions without them biting you when you are afraid of them. Those animals are spirits, when they see you as a greater spirit, they will flee.

The witches are casting their spells on us every time and they would not work because greater is He that is in us than what they have. We are more than conquerors, and overcomers in this world. Praise God!

"And these signs shall follow them that believe; In my name shall they cast out devils; they shall speak with new tongues; They shall take up serpent; and if they drink any deadly thing, it shall not hurt them; they shall lay hands on the sick, and they shall recover." Mark 16:17-18 (KJV).

Simon Peter followed Jesus because he toiled all night without catching a fish. It happened that way because a miracle was on its way. Your disappointment shall turn out to be an appointment for you.

When Christ spoke to him, he cast his net and caught so many fish that his net was giving way and he called for help because they could not bring the net into the boat. His disappointment led him, he cry to the Lord who showed him mercy, signs and wonders.

It was a big miracle for him because fishing is usually done at night, and nothing could be caught in the day. But at the word of the Master, he saw the miracle in the daylight which was part of the sign.

Jesus the Word of God spoke into the river and the fishes rushed to the net. Peter followed Him because of that miracle. The multitudes were following Jesus because they were seeing the miracles He was performing.

Peter and John healed a lame on the beautiful gate and the man rejoiced and followed them into the temple to worship God because he received his miracle. He never bothered to ask them to take him into the temple, but only at the gate to beg for alms before his healing. Many people are defined by their limitations and would not bother to do anything to get out of that limitation like the layman at the beautiful gate.

We need to pray for more anointing of the Holy Ghost so that the enemies cannot overcome us:

- Lord Jesus, thank You for the anointing of overcoming the enemies.
- Thank You, Lord, for opening our eyes to see what others could not see.
- Lord, let your miracle signs and wonders follow us throughout all generations, in the same way Peter and John received their anointing to heal the man at the beautiful gate.
- Lord. thank You for the grace of trampling over the serpent and scorpions and nothing shall hurt us.
- The enemies cannot overcome Your children.
- Thank You, Lord, for if we eat or drink poisonous things, they cannot harm us.
- Let Your blood reign in us.
- Let the thirsty, drink Your living water and the hungry eat the living bread.
- Let Your glory cover the earth as the waters cover the seas.
- Let Thy light shine through Your servants.
- Satisfy all our needs according to Your riches in glory.
- Lord, let Your Holy name be exalted forever, in Jesus' Mighty name! Amen!

A New Person

Any believer does not live for himself but for Christ whom he has given his life. He becomes a new creature in Christ and old things had to pass away and all things have become new.

"Therefore, if any man is in Christ, he is a new creature: old things are passed away; behold, all things have become new." 2 Corinthians 5:17 (KJV).

Following a new creature in Christ, certain signs shall follow him because he is no longer an ordinary but an extraordinary person. By faith, we can get away with many things, even trample on the witches and their witchcraft and it shall not hurt us. Praise God!

"There was a man of the Pharisees, named Nicodemus, a ruler of the Jews: The same came to Jesus by night, and said unto him, Rabbi, we know that thou art a teacher come from God: for no man can do these miracles that thou does, except God be with him. Jesus answered and said unto him, Verily, verily, I say unto thee,

Except a man is born again, he cannot see the kingdom of God. Nicodemus saith unto him, how can a man be born when he is old? can he enter the second time into his mother's womb, and be born? Jesus answered, Verily, verily, I say unto thee, except a man be born of water and the Spirit, he cannot enter the kingdom of God. That which is born of the flesh is flesh, and that which is born of the Spirit is spirit." John 3:1-6 (KJV).

Now let us dissect the above paragraph and determine what it means to be a new creature in Christ and a born again. They are the same. In the case of Uncle Nicodemus, he was looking at the miracles of King Jesus and His level of wisdom. He knew that the Hand of the Lord was upon Him, hence he went to him in the night. He went in the night, why not in the day?

He did not mention the kingdom in his question, but the Lord knew his mind hence He told him "That a man cannot enter the kingdom of God except, he is born again." King Jesus used the phrase 'born again' while Apostle Paul used the term 'new creature.'

Although our Lord taught through parables, in clear terms, He taught Uncle Nicodemus that he cannot get into the Kingdom of God without a kingdom mindset. You cannot be what you are until you become what you are or what you want to be. You can only be in the kingdom when you set your mind on it and believe it to be true. Take for example the Lord was getting miracles because He believes in miracles, otherwise, it would have been impossible for him to do them.

Miracles cannot go to those who do not believe in miracles but look for those who are looking for them. You cannot get what you do not have because everything good or evil is created in your heart. The Father is a miracle, King Jesus is another miracle, and we are also miracles, and products of signs and wonders. It is much easier to get your miracles when you know about them and believe in them.

Your reality could be an illusion because it is created in your heart, and you have the power to change it if you do not want it. If you are broke, you can take to heart that Christ was rich and was made poor so that we might become rich. "Though the Lord Jesus Christ was rich, yet for your sake He became poor, that you through His poverty might become rich." 2 Corinthians 8:9 (KJV).

If you are sick, you must take comfort that Christ took many strips so that we do not get sick. Remember also that He took our sins and He who knew no sin was made sin so that we might become the righteousness of God. Therefore, where sin abounds, grace abounds the more. When it comes to death, He has already died for us and conquered death for us and it has no strings on us. It is a belief system.

If you believe in the promise of prosperity, your thought system will help you to find a way to create that wealth even if you are poor. In the same way, your heart will help you to keep well if you believe in staying well and the same applies to life and death.

I saw a man who talks about sickness all the time you see him. One of the days, I had to pray for him and ask him to stop thinking and talking about sickness after this prayer because I knew the Lord touched him. Some days or weeks passed, and I saw him and he said, 'Since I stopped thinking of sickness, I have been well.'

Your new person is in you when you believe. Your salvation is in you. He has already declared that if we believe, we cannot taste death and if we have already died, we shall come back to life. Anybody can go to the kingdom of God, but he must have that kingdom mentality or mindset.

Apostle Paul was emphasizing the 'born again' of Jesus when he was teaching the doctrine of a new creation. You do not have to go back to your mother's womb as taught by the Lord Jesus but requires renewal of your mind. It is the reinvention of oneself through thoughts and mind development.

A new spirit in a new mindset. You need to be born with water which is used for cleansing and the Spirit which is the power of God living in you. Before you can become that born-again or new creature, you must renew your mind by going through the process of retraining your mind from the old which was filled with fears, doubts, corruption and negativity. It is a total cleansing and a change of mindset.

A born-again or new creature has renewed his mind or thinking. He has developed a mental attitude like the Apostle Paul, who mimicked Christ in all his ways. The man of God who created a niche of faith for himself is worth emulation. After his encounter with the Lord at Damascus, he became a born again of the Spirit before the water which cleansed him from the blood of the saints which they shed.

He became a disciple and shepherd from his old way of persecuting the same. When the Lord touched him, he became a new creature and stopped looking and seeing things from his old way but looking at them from a different perspective and seeing differently.

This is because there is no way you can see differently when you continue to look at the same thing with the same eyes in the same manner. To be a new person, you must develop your heart because it is in the heart. You must create a new belief system because there is no way you can get to the kingdom of God without being born again or creating the kingdom mentality in you.

Your heart is the engine that drives your life, you must focus your mind on the kingdom of God to be able to get to the kingdom. You fashion it the way you would want to live, success or failure, heaven, or hell. "A good man out of the good treasure of his heart bringeth forth that which is good, and an evil man out of the evil treasure of his heart bringeth forth that which is evil: for of the abundance of the heart his mouth speaks." Luke 6:45 (KJV).

Prayer Against the Witches

"For the Lord, your God is a consuming fire, a jealous God." Deuteronomy 4:24 (AV). "As fire consumes the forest, and as the flame sets the mountains ablaze, so pursue and afflict them with Your tempest and terrify them with Your tornado or hurricane" Psalm 83:14-15 (AV).

Say this prayer to destroy any evil satellite they have built to monitor and transmit information about you for their evil purposes:

- Lord, I know that you use winds as your messenger and flames of fire as your minister, send them to go and destroy any evil satellite they are using to transmit information about me.

- Lord, I know that you are a God of consuming fire; let Your fire consume any evil gathering where our names are mentioned.
- Let the Holy Ghost fire consume anything that tends to delay or kill my destiny.
- Anywhere they call our names for evil, let the Holy Ghost fire and thunder answer them and lick them up like the burnt offering of Elijah.
- Thank you, Lord, for answering me, in Jesus' name, Amen.

*Available worldwide from Amazon
and all good bookstores*

www.mtp.agency

mtp.agency

@mtp_agency

www.ingramcontent.com/pod-product-compliance
Lightning Source LLC
LaVergne TN
LVHW051218070526
838200LV00064B/4963